Practical Excellence

A hands-on guide to obtaining Sustainable Excellence
through using the EFQM Excellence Model and
participation in related Global Business Awards

Chris Hakes

About Practical Good Practice Guides

This book is one of a series of collaborations between Chris Hakes at Leadership Agenda Limited and Geoff Carter at PacePerformance Limited. Chris and Geoff spent the formative part of their respective careers in operational and general management roles in large international organisations and became passionate about sustaining the performance of their organisations through focussed continual improvement and innovation. They were part of the first wave of practitioners who supported the formation of the EFQM over 20 years ago and, to this day, they remain key players in the international Excellence community. They have helped several National and Regional Awards (based on the EFQM Model) to form and develop and have experienced a unique and privileged perspective on Excellence through their training and assessing of those trying to attain it, they are both members of the "EFQM Faculty" in Brussels.

This book is the first of several good practice Guides. Soon to be released publications include "Practical Strategy" by Geoff Carter and "Practical Innovation" by Chris Hakes. Make sure that www.leadershipagenda. com is in your "favourites" list so that you can check on launch dates for the other Guides in this series. You can also sign up now for newsletters at this web site and guarantee to be informed as soon as they become available.

Colophon

Title	Practical Excellence - A hands-on, good practice guide to obtaining Sustainable Excellence through using the EFQM Excellence Model and participation in related Global Business Awards.
Author	Chris Hakes.
Editorial Review	Geoff Carter.
Publisher	Leadership Agenda Limited, UK.
ISBN (13)	978-1-904861-01-0
Print	First edition September 2011.

Copyright

The aim of this book is to enhance the "standardised" framework of the Model with practical insight, so aside from the high level criteria/concept descriptions, all other content in this book, including the examples of proven good practices in the template pages (that enable readers to learn from what leaders in Award winning excellent organisations have done), are the work and views of the Author(s) with copyright being assigned to the publisher, '© Leadership Agenda Limited, UK. 2011'

Content Nature and Advised Use

This is not an academic text, the approaches advised in this book are concise in description (we do not elaborate in detailed justifications) and practical; they are informed by hands-on experiences of working with and analysing the success of several EFQM Excellence Award winners, and a very broad range of organisations in the Public Sector. We have tried to publish this book in the practical language of 'business' but in a way, which we hope and believe, will be relevant to all organisations, public or private, large or small. Clearly not all practices described will be relevant for all organisations and we must warn readers of a need to also rely on applying common sense to contextualise the practices described and verify their relevance to their own organisation.

September 2011, Leadership Agenda Limited, UK.

Contents

How to use this book

Of course, use it any way it helps you, but there is a little logic you might like to be aware of, we suggest:

- Start with a quick flick through (scan) of the whole book to **get a feel for the layout and content.**

- Read sections 1 to 5., so as to **be clear on what Sustainable Excellence is and why Assessments or Award Submissions may be able to help you.** Perhaps debate these sections with your colleagues? Maybe visit a few organisations or conferences to get a feel for what others have achieved?

- Dive deep into section 6 and follow its seven proven steps to **create detailed plans and learn of Assessment Good Practices.**

- **Start Assessing** by using the proforma templates in section 7 to help you prepare and undertake assessments.

- **Reflect on what others have achieved** by reading section 8

1. Introduction and Acknowledgements

Yet again, for a long time I was determined not to write another book. For many years, in the period 1993 to 2007, I authored publications on the techniques of 'Corporate Self-Assessment', first published by Chapman and Hall, and then by Blackwell's and later, in different forms, by others, all now out of print and dated, in my mind by their titles alone (please do not buy them!). Those books contained overviews of the history and evolution of what were then called Business Excellence Models and were designed to help EFQM and others promote the value and practical use of their "Excellence" performance measurement systems.

Looking back over the last 20 years it is clear now that the EFQM and others have been very successful with the global growth and use of their performance models but that the ways in which some organisations have chosen to apply these models is very flawed. Many organisations are at risk of a great waste of time, effort, resource and opportunity in the ways in which they pursue Sustainable Excellence and this is often caused by the lack of, or poor quality of advice they have received.

This is intended to be a "self-help" book and is an attempt to help organisations and their leaders to pursue Sustainable Excellence in a more efficient and effective way. It is also, for those who wish to, a way to help them to apply to win Excellence Awards (such as the EFQM Excellence Award or National or Regional variants of it). Performance Awards that can robustly assess and recognise progress with Sustainable Excellence seem to be having a resurgence, perhaps driven by the need of Regions and Nations to rebuild performance and ensure they are maintaining globally productive, post crisis, diversified relevant economies. Such Excellence or Performance Awards, if based on sound models and assessment processes, can help organisations develop long-term prosperity but the risks of poor or little advice remain, particularly if inappropriate or ineffective consultancy support is obtained when making Award applications. I hope this book may help a little to put some focus on overcoming such issues.

I could not have done this book alone and I would like to acknowledge and thank all those who have assisted, persisted, influenced, or generally helped to maintain my sanity during the production of this book and most importantly my sometime business partner and colleague at the EFQM Faculty, Geoff Carter. Geoff's deep experiences of the Excellence model have contributed to a variety of other books and publications over many years. His personal Excellence journey has been enriched through professional relationships with members of many Global Performance Excellence programmes. He has supported successive EFQM CEO's at the "GEM Council". (The Global Excellence Model Council members are the guardians of the premier Excellence Models across the world. Through a formalised approach for sharing their knowledge, experience and information, the GEM Council serves as a global fraternity in the field of Excellence. Take a look at https://sites.google.com/site/globalexcellencemodels/home for more insights) and I am deeply indebted to having his support in editing and reviewing this publication. His enthusiasm to help leaders, managers and practitioners to navigate their own journey to Sustainable Excellence is endless.

Also, particular thanks are due to all other friends and colleagues at EFQM and other Global or Regional Awards administrations with whom my own learning journey has always been a two-way experience and, for me at least, a great pleasure. This book is a collection of proven practices, based on these privileged experiences.

Finally, I'd like to note that I make no academic or research-based claims for this work, nor do I suggest exclusivity of thinking for the ideas tabled here; all I can assure you is that there are many users of the EFQM Excellence Model and several winners of the EFQM Excellence Award who have benefited from learning of the proven good practices listed in the pro-forma tools (and elsewhere in the book) and finding effective ways to assess their progress against them. It is an old saying that, 'there is no finish-line in the race to Excellence –the race never ends'. Sometimes, however, it is important for some (be they Individuals, Organisations, Regions or Governments) to remember to begin the race and for others to renew the vigour and effectiveness with which they compete. I really hope this book may help you to begin or renew your journey to Sustainable Excellence.

Chris Hakes, Cambridge UK, September 2011

2. Why is Sustainable Excellence important?

In order to maintain successful economies, Organisations, Regions and Nations need to be both globally productive and able to sustain their performance in increasingly uncertain strategic environments. Most leaders cannot predict the future, but they can act to improve their organisation's efficiency, effectiveness, foresight and agility in order to build entities that will survive and flourish under just about any possible future.

Standing still is no longer an option, whatever an organisation does today will be out of date tomorrow, so every strategy, process or person of an organisation and its alliances must be subject to continual review, acquisition of new knowledge/learning, innovation and improvement. Sustainably successful organisations maintain their success by continually challenging the status quo of the ways in which they operate and taking practical and innovative steps to make the required changes.

Over the last half century a range of techniques, some collectively titled under "Quality" or "Excellence" or "Customer" or "People" or "Sustainability" or "Social Responsibility" or such like banners have come to the fore to support such aims. If done well they can add very significant value to organisations, but equally, for many, they can (if implemented in ill-advised ways) create ineffective and bureaucratic processes and become a restraint, not an advantage, for the organisation involved. The challenge is to know how to get it right and how to integrate all of these efforts.

One proven way of doing this is by creating a clear Vision of what "Sustainable Excellence" means in practice (to have a clear aspiration) and then to engage the organisation and its key stakeholders in making and reviewing progress to that aim. This can help Leaders in the organisation to communicate and develop a culture where Excellence is the norm and employees become more agile, productive, motivated and engaged in the changes needed.

Organisations can, of course, create their own unique visions of what Sustainable Excellence means but there are advantages in applying proven Excellence frameworks created by others. Chapters 3 and 4 introduce one of the most commonly used holistic performance frameworks, the EFQM Excellence Model, and highlight some of the advantages of basing your performance tracking on a common model applied throughout the organisation; in particular that you will have a globally common "language" for sharing and learning performance insights from/with others.

By using performance models focussed on Sustainable Excellence, organisations around the world, be they small or large, public or private, enjoy many benefits as a result of applying Excellence centric techniques to track their progress, these include:

- a fact-based technique for **Assessing an Organisation's Strengths and Areas for Improvement** and then measuring its progress, based on an holistic analysis of stakeholder insights, perceptions and achievements;

- a way to understand the **Coherency and Depth of Strategy Implementation**, helping to integrate the various projects and Improvement Initiatives that may exist;

- a way to **Compare Performance with Others and Identify Good Practices**, both internally and externally;

- a basis for creating a **Common Vocabulary,** way of thinking and method to educate people in continual improvement;

- a way to draw from and co-ordinate the **Contributions of all Stakeholders**; and

- a way to pull all of the above together in order to **Conclude and Target what Changes/Innovations will be needed to Deliver Desired Future Performance.**

3. How can we define Sustainable Excellence for our organisation?

A good starting place is to apply the proven thinking of others. Using a proven framework gives you a common language by which to share and learn with others. Thousands of organisations, around the globe, have applied the EFQM Excellence Model and associated tools and good practices to energise themselves to learn, share and innovate. EFQM, the Brussels based non-profit management association that owns this most commonly used framework (See Appendix 1 for details), defines an excellent organisation as follows:

"Excellent organisations achieve and sustain superior levels of performance that meet or exceed the expectations of all their stakeholders".

To fully understand this definition of Sustainable Excellence the meaning of each word is important, particular note should be made of the context of the use of the following words:

"Achieving" Excellence is one thing, **"sustaining"** it is another level of challenge; it means that superior performance must be seen to be maintained over time.

"Superior" is a contextual word, where context is given by reviewing performance both quantitatively and qualitatively, with competitors and proven leading edge organisations both from the same sphere as your organisation and from other sectors

"All stakeholders" brings added meaning, it is not just about meeting or exceeding the expectations of one stakeholder group but, for long term success, a balance must be obtained with all groups with a vested interest in the success of the organisation (i.e. its "Owners", its Customers, its People and the Society in which it operates).

So far so good, you may now have your own definition of Excellence, you may even have some views on the values and behaviours that should underpin it, but all this is not enough unless you can target, act upon and measure relevant and real change.

To get from the simple, but useful, definition on the previous page, to a robust performance assessment model, EFQM consulted with, and has continually engaged representative organisations globally. The outcomes of this engagement have been:

- To create and maintain views on the principles, values and beliefs that EFQM believes represents a consensus view of what will underpin progress towards Sustainable Excellence. EFQM call these the **Fundamental Concepts** of Excellence and these are introduced below.

- To create an assessment framework and measurement system. EFQM calls these the **EFQM Model and RADAR** and these are described in Chapters 4 and 7.

EFQM's Eight Concepts of Excellence are:

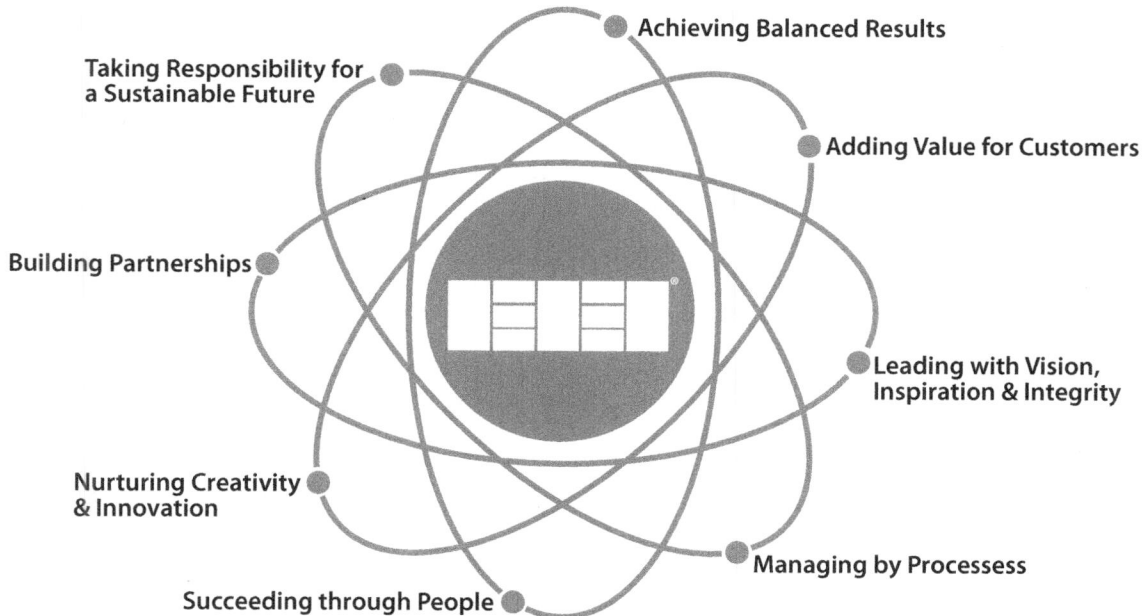

Achieving Balanced Results

Taking Responsibility for a Sustainable Future

Adding Value for Customers

Building Partnerships

Leading with Vision, Inspiration & Integrity

Nurturing Creativity & Innovation

Managing by Processess

Succeeding through People

So Eight Fundamental Concepts of Sustainable Excellence, that you could review and use are:

Achieving Balanced Results

Excellent organisations meet their Mission and progress towards their Vision through planning and achieving a balanced set of results that meet both the short and long term needs of their stakeholders and, where relevant, exceed them.

Adding Value for Customers

Excellent organisations know that customers are their primary reason for being and strive to innovate and create value for them by understanding and anticipating their needs and expectations.

Leading with Vision, Inspiration & Integrity

Excellent organisations have leaders who shape the future and make it happen, acting as role models for its Values and Ethics.

Managing by Processes

Excellent organisations are managed through structured and strategically aligned processes using fact-based decision making to create balanced and sustained results.

Succeeding through People

Excellent organisations value their people and create a culture of empowerment for the balanced achievement of organisational and personal goals.

Nurturing Creativity & Innovation

Excellent organisations generate increased value and levels of performance through continual and systematic innovation by harnessing the creativity of their stakeholders.

Building Partnerships

Excellent organisations seek, develop and maintain trusting relationships with various partners to ensure mutual success. These partnerships may be formed with customers, society, key suppliers, educational bodies or Non-Governmental Organisations (NGO's).

Taking Responsibility for a Sustainable Future

Excellent organisations embed within their culture an ethical mind-set; clear Values and the highest standards for organisational behaviour, all of which enable them to strive for economic, social and ecological sustainability.

These concepts underpin the EFQM Excellence Model and were created by EFQM in the early 1990s; they were then, and continue to be, informed and renewed by their networks and users. They thereby represent a consensus on the key management principles and beliefs on what will drive the sustainable success of organisations. The EFQM Excellence Model itself (see Chapters 4 and 7) is simply a framework to translate these concepts into action.

For an organisation to maximise the benefits of adopting the EFQM Excellence Model, a management team must first ensure that it is comfortable with these concepts. Clearly, if these concepts are not fully understood and accepted then progress will be difficult and potentially meaningless.

A booklet with further insights on the EFQM's Fundamental Concepts can be downloaded from www.efqm.org

4. How can we Manage and Measure "Sustainable Excellence"?

The EFQM Excellence Model translates the eight previously described Fundamental Concepts of management into a dynamic and non-prescriptive operational model, by which performance can be assessed. It defines "what" has to be managed in an organisation (the "Criterion") and "how" they should be managed and measured (via a tool called "RADAR")

If used well, measurement with such models, can help organisations, public and private, small and large, assess their performance against globally developed frameworks and adapt their performance to changing global realities.

In it's simplest form, the **EFQM Excellence Model** is a 9-box "Cause and Effect" diagram.

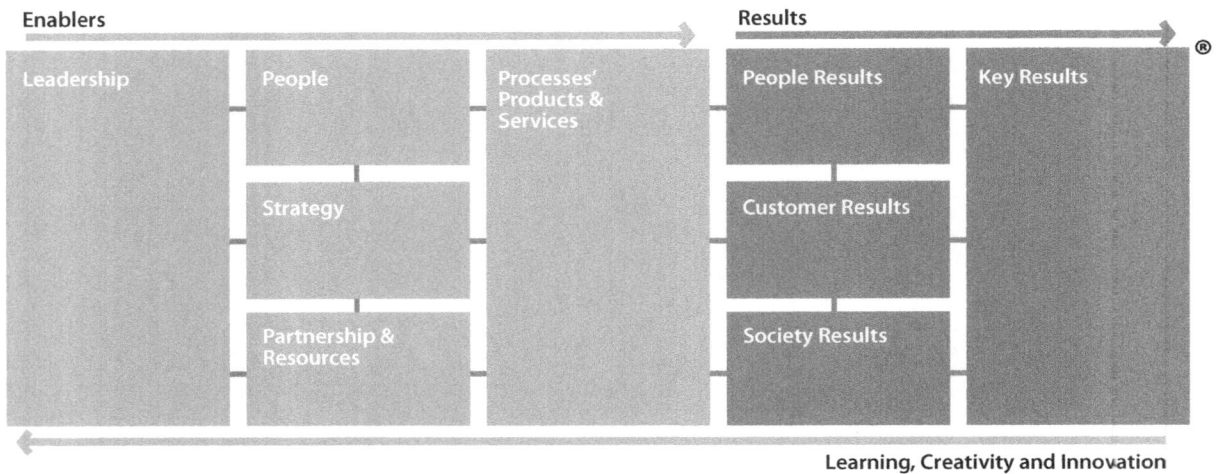

Enablers   **Results**   ®

Leadership	People	Processes' Products & Services	People Results	Key Results
	Strategy		Customer Results	
	Partnership & Resources		Society Results	

Learning, Creativity and Innovation

It contains:

Five key **Enablers** of Sustainable Excellence (1. Leadership, 2. Strategy, 3. People, 4. Partnership and Resources and 5. Processes, Product and Services), shown on the left in the diagram.

   - These criteria provide ways to assess both what is being done and how it is being done in the organisation, which, if done efficiently and effectively, should be dynamically driving Excellence in

The four **Results** criteria (6. Customers, 7. People, 8. Society and 9. Key Results), shown on the right in the diagram.

   - These criteria provide ways to give context to what has been achieved with/for all the organisation's stakeholders.

To sustainably improve the Results it achieves, an organisation must assess and improve what it does (the Enablers). In this context the Model is dynamic, the diagram above shows arrows moving from Enablers to Results, left to right (cause to desired effect), and then with "Learning, Creativity and Innovation" back, right to left, to close a learning loop by reviewing the Enablers in the light of what they achieved). A tool called RADAR is used to put data and logic to these assessments. We will revisit this when we get to RADAR later, in Chapter 7, but for now it is just important to note the that the Model and RADAR logic demands that innovation and learning must be present to continually refine and improve the Enablers that will, in turn, be likely to lead to further improved future Results.

Beneath each of the nine criteria in the Model framework is a set of Criterion-parts. There are x32 in total, 24 for Enablers, 8 for Results.

An example follows for the Leadership Criterion, showing the x5 Criterion-parts 1a to 1e. (All x32 are fully described in section 7). These Criterion-parts collectively provide a more detailed description of the Model and a framework by which performance can be targeted and evaluated. In an Award Assessment, x32 scoring decisions are made by a team of qualified Assessors.

Example of Criterion Structure: -Leadership Criterion 1

Each Criterion starts with an introductory aspirational statement; for Leadership this is:

"**Excellent organisations have leaders who** shape the future and make it happen, acting as role models for its values and ethics and inspiring trust at all times. They are flexible, enabling the organisation to anticipate and react in a timely manner to ensure the on-going success of the organisation".

Each criterion is then segmented into a number of criterion-parts. The example below shows the segmentation of the Leadership Criterion of the EFQM Excellence Model. The "Enabler Mapping" and "Result Mapping" assessment proforma's in section 7 of this book, highlight all the Criterion-parts linked to each of the 9 Criterion and we encourage you to scan these pages now, noting in particular the content and layout of the x9 flow diagrams that describe the Criterion-parts.

There are **5 Criterion-part assessments** for Leadership, these are:

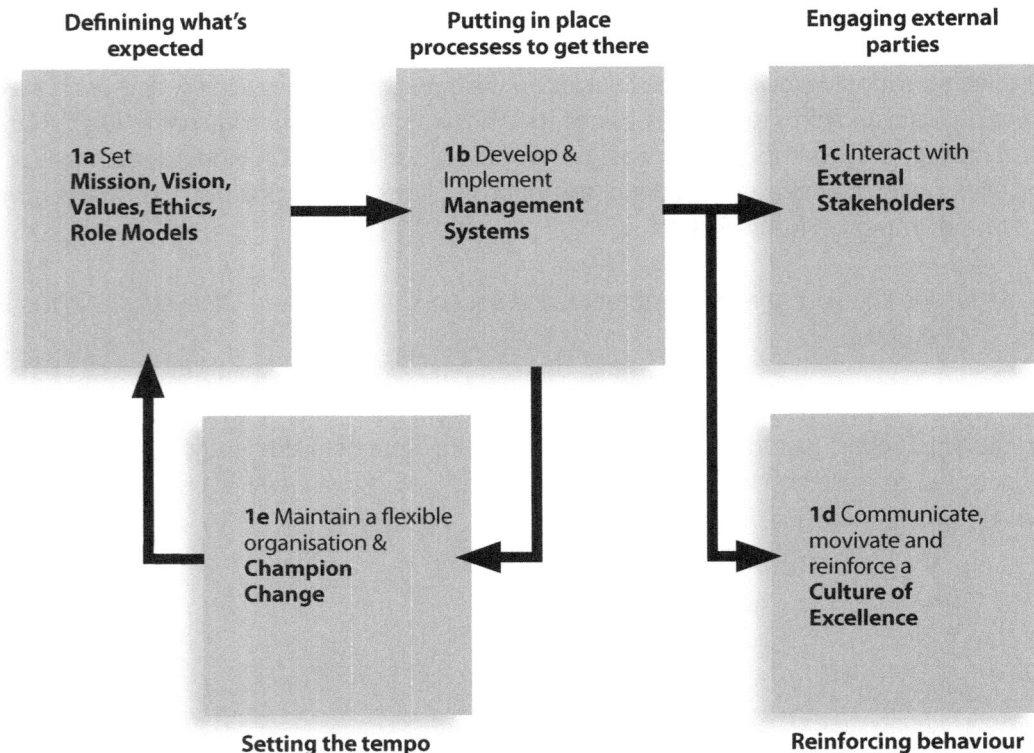

Defining what's expected	Putting in place processess to get there	Engaging external parties
1a Set **Mission, Vision, Values, Ethics, Role Models**	**1b** Develop & Implement **Management Systems**	**1c** Interact with **External Stakeholders**
1e Maintain a flexible organisation & **Champion Change**		**1d** Communicate, movivate and reinforce a **Culture of Excellence**
Setting the tempo		Reinforcing behaviour

5. What's involved if we Apply to Win Awards? Should we do it?

Is it for you?

You can apply the EFQM Model and obtain business benefits without applying to win Awards and many organisations do (you create your own performance evidence records and assess them yourselves). However, applying to win Awards can play an extremely valuable part in accelerating change programmes. Organisations who can demonstrate enduring Excellence have almost invariably learnt to participate in global networks and use the insights gained from such practices to hone on-going improvements of the efficiency and effectiveness of their organisation and Regions. Going through the Assessment process of an Excellence Award can help leaders robustly track their progress and bring valuable external perspectives and learning, as well as, potentially, enabling them to be recognised for their achievements.

However it is important that the use of "Awards" be seen as an integral part of a programme of change or organisational development, not an end in itself. Successful users of Award processes normally link their use of them to their own strategic planning cycles, rather than just entering with an aspirational "hope" for getting some recognition that they believe may have personal or organisational promotion value.

Care should be exercised with the setting of stretching but realistic goals for Award achievements, rather than just aspirational promotional or "winning" targets. For successful users of Awards the 'gems" they seek are not the Awards themselves, rather it's the performance evaluations and networking connections they provide as part of the Award process.

What's Involved?

There are now, globally, an estimated 30-40 National or Regional Awards that are based on the EFQM Excellence Model. The size and nature of these Award processes varies (as EFQM does not control them "tightly") but it is common that a team of trained and experienced Assessors is assigned (up to 8 assessors for large Applicants) to your Assessment project and that three common process stages will be followed. These are:

Stage 1: Pre site visit sharing and planning

Prior to a site visit (see stage 2), and to typically fixed and immovable annual cycles/deadlines, the applicant organisation prepares a portfolio of performance and process evidence to give to the Assessors to help them form initial views and to be able to plan a site visit. The format for this is normally prescribed and is, typically, either:

1 A so-called "Submission Document" of up to 75 pages of A4 narrative, charts and diagrams formatted to reflect the Results and Enablers of the organisations performance against the 9 Criterion of the EFQM Model or,

2   A so-called "Enabler Map" and "Qualification File" document pack that lists, more simply, the Enabler practices that exist and the high level Results they achieve. With this process the Assessors then add more "flesh" when on site based on the framework of practices and results described.

As option 2 places significantly increased demands on Assessor teams, it is important to note that, at present, the only Award process that allows applicants to use Enabler Maps and Qualification files (i.e. option 2 above), is the EFQM's own Excellence Award process, although this will likely change over time.

The pre-site visit work as an Award Assessor starts when the Assessor team receives the Submission Document. Each Assessor analyses   the document and familiarises him/herself with the organisation and its stated performance. The team then meets and under the leadership of an Assessment Team Leader, comes to a common view on their high level understanding of the organisation, the key features of its performance and most importantly the outline of a site visit plan. –The things the team will wish to verify and clarify when they arrive on site.

Subsequently the Team Leader, in partnership with the Applicant, will conclude the logistics and other practicalities for a site visit.

Stage 2: Site Visit

The duration of the site visit stage varies according to the nature of the organisation (size, sites, etc.) or the Award process, but is often to the order of 3-5 days on site and involves the whole Assessor team.

After an opening meeting with the senior management team, a typical format will be for the Assessor team to split up to undertake a series of meetings, normally working in pairs. This will nearly invariably include a mixture of small team meetings, data reviews, interviews and lower down the organisation, discussion groups. The specific nature of the discussions they hold will be framed by the team's reviews of the points they wish to clarify/verify after their analysis of the document provided in stage 1. i.e. the Submission Document.

An important feature of a site visit is that they are not scheduled to 100% interview/meeting capacity on each day. A sound and typical site visit process is iterative. At the end of each day, the Assessor team will meet; share their findings to date on perceived Strengths and Areas for Improvement per Criterion-part and review with the Applicant any new, revised or rescheduled meetings that maybe needed.

Both Assessors and Applicants need to devote significant time to preparing for and managing the site visit process, if it is to be effective in realistically assessing the Applicants achievements and giving them valuable feedback.

Stage 3: Post Site Visit and Feedback

The last step consists of creating and delivering a so-called "Feedback Report" to the Applicant, which also goes in parallel (in most Award processes) to an independent Jury Review Board who are tasked to to make final Award recognition decisions.

The Feedback Report is based on the analysis of the Strengths and Areas for Improvement as analysed during the site visit along with the Assessor team's consensus view of how the Applicant scores against the EFQM Model and RADAR (See also Chapters 7 and 8 for more insights on RADAR and scoring). In most Award processes, the Feedback report will contain the following sections:

- A brief overview of the process followed for assessing all the applications for the Award;
- An executive summary;
- Detailed +/- comments relating to each of the x32 Model Criterion-parts (from 1a to 9b as described in the flow diagrams in Section 7 of this book);
- The score achieved within bands of 10 percentage points for the x32 Criterion-parts and the overall score achieved in intervals of 50 points on the scale 0 -1000 using the weighted points of the Model (as described in Section 7 of this book).

6. Seven Proven Steps for Benefiting from Self-Assessment or Award Submissions

Whether you are making an Award submission or simply gathering data for a simpler in-house Self-Assessment (i.e. using your own managers or teams to assess) there are common good practices that you can learn from and these are summarised in the following seven good practice steps.

In outline they are:

Step 1   Agree and **Share the Aims**
(What do you want to obtain from doing the Assessment?)

Step 2   Get **"Everyone on board"**

Step 3   Frame the **Scope and Strategic Context** of the Assessment
(Make sure the Assessors understand it too!)

Step 4   **Assign Roles, Responsibilities and Accountabilities**
(-Maybe not just for the Assessment project but on-going too?)

Step 5   Create a **Sound Plan**
(Including information gathering, documenting your performance and preparing for Site Visits or Self-Assessments)

Step 6   Spot and Overcome **Typical Road-Blocks**
(-Manage your plan and do it without consultants?)

Step 7   Prepare for and use the **Feedback Report**
(Acting on the outcomes of your Self-Assessment)

Step **1**

Agree and Share the Aims
(What do you want to obtain from doing the Assessment?)

Some organisations apply to win Awards because they have to, others because they want to. For whatever reason you became engaged with the Award process you will, if you do it well, invest a significant (but highly valuable) amount of time in preparing for the Award analysis and you would be wise to have a clear view, in your organisation, as to why you are doing this and how you are going to use the Assessment outcomes.

Although your answer to the question 'why are we doing this?' may change over time (as you become more experienced and robust with your assessments), it is a good practice to maintain clarity with this important point and to ensure it is communicated to your People and other key stakeholders.

Organisations enjoy many potential benefits as a result of undertaking assessments using the EFQM Excellence Model, some have been touched on in previous sections, the following list is not a checklist or even a suggestion for you, but it does example some of the reasons often given by Applicants that may help you conclude your own thinking. These include:

- "Winning and obtaining the associated recognition/promotion" (Nice if you really are that good....).
- "Understanding your Organisation's Strengths and Areas for Improvement and being able to track and target progress".
- "Comparing your performance with others and being able to learn".
- "Knowing where to target your seeking of Global Good Practices".
- "Providing momentum for your change initiatives by using the assessment to help create and embed a Common Vocabulary for Sustainable Excellence".
- "Providing a way to draw from and communicate to all Stakeholders in a way that enhances mutual learning and understanding of your performance".

It is also always essential that Managers at all levels in the organisation are fully engaged in, and understand the benefits of, the Award engagement. It is not a process for a specialist team, person, project, consultant or department, who, alone, will at worst just create a presentational pack of Award Submission documents and thereby obtain an Assessment that is not based on reality and unable to help you with your real performance improvement needs.

Step 2

Get "Everyone on board"

As said previously, done well, this is not a process that can be delegated to a specialist team, person, project, consultant or department. If you proceed in such an isolated manner you are highly unlikely to undertake a robust assessment and will miss out on a great opportunity to improve the effectiveness of how you drive long term change, if you do not seek the broad engagement of your people in the goal of Sustainable Excellence.

So, for most good practice Award Applications or Self-Assessment cycles, you will start with a period of open communication before getting to creation of the documents needed. A sound communication plan will:

- Share the overall objectives and make clear why they are important (see previous Step 1.)
- Make clear what is expected of the recipient(s) –Those being communicated to.
- Describe how you intend to handle the feedback at the end of the Award Application or Self-Assessment.
- Be on-going and regularly updated.

Part of the challenge of getting organisational momentum through broad engagement of your people and other stakeholders, is to get everyone to understand Sustainable Excellence in the same way. The EFQM Fundamental Concepts, Excellence Model and RADAR are most successful when they have the support and understanding (in different ways, at different levels) of everyone in the organisation.

To achieve this, a systematic plan for raising awareness (of the Concepts/Model/RADAR) is often useful and could include:

- Visits or conferences to meet face-to face with executives and/or organisations who have been using the Model for some time;
- Telling stories of Excellence from outside, especially by your Leadership Team;
- Providing reading materials, such as those published by EFQM and or translations made by National or Regional Award schemes using the EFQM Excellence Model (See Appendix 1 of this book);
- Kick off training/workshops on the EFQM Excellence Model/the Fundamental Concepts/Your Aims;
- Circulating copies of published Award-winning submissions if you can obtain them;

- Having some of your managers participate in the Assessment of other organisations. The purpose of this is partly to raise their knowledge of the Model and RADAR but also for them to have the opportunity to learn about good practice in other organisations and to signal that you are serious about learning about Excellence.
- RADARISE (See section 7. of this book) your management practices, i.e. role model the use of RADAR, by using it in daily management, for example in meetings you could:
    - Insist they are always started with expressions like 'What will success look like?', 'What decision are we looking for?', 'What are you trying to get out of this meeting?'
    - Review the efficiency and effectiveness of every meeting by asking; 'Did we start on time?', 'Did we work effectively?', 'Did we get what we wanted from the meeting?', 'Could we have run that meeting/discussion better?' in order to stimulate improvements.

Step 3

Frame the Scope and Strategic Context of the Assessment
(and make sure the Assessors understand it too..)

Right at the start of the project, it is essential to scope the assessment by defining the boundaries of the organisation to be assessed and by being clear on the strategic context for the assessment.

You need to do this in a formal way and ensure the Assessors (be they for the Award, or internal Self-Assessment) have understood it. A good way of doing this is to articulate your position on 5 so-called "Key Factors" that are used by several Award administrations to help Assessors frame the Award Assessments.

For some organisations this maybe very straightforward but it is essential that the Assessors see these key factors the same way as you do. For others, it may be more difficult, for example, if your organisation is a Division or Sub-Unit within a larger enterprise, with full accountability for some of its activities, but taking some of its internal services from the parent company; then the answers to some of the following 'Key Factors' maybe complex. Either way open, honest, transparency is essential if you are to obtain a focussed and value adding assessment.

There are typically five Key Factors that you are asked to confidentially respond to with a positioning/framing insight. Your responses to these Key Factors are not in themselves judged, but are used to frame the context within which the EFQM Model and RADAR are applied.

For instance if you respond to KF5 (see following section) with a statement such as "One of our key challenges/growth areas will be to introduce the innovative new "XYZ" service" then the Assessors will contextualise how they interpret the EFQM Model and RADAR with this statement of relative importance in mind. For example, in the scenario just created, in criterion-part 5c, which is an assessment about how you Promote and Market your Products and Services, (see also Section 7.) they will likely want to see the specific approaches related to communicating the value proposition of the "XYZ" service. Also, in the Results criteria, particularly 6. "Customer results" and 9. "Key, or business, results", they will expect to see outcomes that allow the performance of the "XYZ" service to be understood.

The five Key Factor (KF) areas, against each of which you should write positioning/framing statement for the Assessment are:

KF1: -Organisational definition/environment

Where you should share a short list of the facts that define your organisation: Its history, Values, Vision and Mission, its geographical sites, people, etc. that you wish the assessment to be framed by.

KF2: -Performance improvement system

A listing of your key approaches to improving the performance of your organisation: i.e. what is the mix of tools that are used? This helps Assessors to understand the basic building blocks of your systems.

KF3: -Organisational relationships

Here you should list those who you regard as current and potential stakeholders: key partners, key suppliers, relationship with parent organisation (if appropriate), internal customer supplier relationships, etc.

KF4: -Competitive environment

Here you openly (but confidentially) list current and potential markets/intermediaries/competitors/customers, your position in different markets, key customer needs, segmentations, major customers, use of distributors, etc.

KF5: -Your main strategic challenges

Finally, but maybe most importantly, list here key risks and opportunities in current and future value propositions: which ones are already achieved, what are the ones ahead in the near and further future.

One way of ensuring you make wise responses to Key Factors is to ensure you have clarity and consensus (in your management teams) on who are your stakeholders and their strategic importance. The EFQM Excellence Model defines a stakeholder as the "Person, group or organisation that has a direct or indirect stake or interest in the organisation because it can either affect the organisation or be affected by it". Within this definition, the following stakeholder sub-groups usually occur:

- **Customers** - Recipients of the products or services provided by the organisation, including if appropriate distributors and intermediaries.
- **People** - All individuals employed by the organisation, whether on a full time, part time or voluntary basis. This includes the leaders of the organisation. If you use contract staff it is important to be clear in the context of the assessment as to whether you support/manage them as "partners" (see below) or as part of your "People".
- **Partners** - Those external parties to the organisation, that you strategically choose to work with, to achieve common objectives and sustained mutual benefit.
- **Society** - The social infrastructure outside the organisation that can be either affected by the organisation, or have an effect on the organisation. For some organisations there is sometimes overlap between "customers" and "community" but it is important to be clear on how you see this.
- **Shareholders or commercial/strategic Stakeholders** - This is the group of stakeholders to whom the leaders of the organisation have responsibility for delivering the organisation's strategy. In private companies, this will be the owners or shareholders. In Operating Units, the organisation's hierarchy will define this group. In the Public Sector, this will usually be the governmental body to which the organisation belongs.

In conclusion it is important that the Executive Management Team (EMT) of the organisation being assessed agree the Key Factors that will frame the Assessment before the organisation makes it's submission or starts its Self-Assessment. In this way all those involved understand the context in which responses should be made when creating the full Submission Document and during site visit interviews.

Step4

Assign Roles, Responsibilities and Accountabilities
(maybe not just for the Assessment project but on-going too?)

It's worth emphasising again, that creating Submission Documents or inputs to a Self-Assessment, that enable your best successes to be realistically assessed, can never be one person's job. As an EFQM assessment is organisation wide and holistic, it is most unlikely that any one individual is likely to have the breadth of knowledge to assemble a comprehensive view, alone.

You can segment or combine the roles suggested below in different ways but a critical dependency/good practice for a successful application is to ensure that all the key tasks/responsibilities detailed in the following sections, are assigned.

Executive Management Team (EMT) responsibilities should always include:

As a minimum the Executive Management Team should be responsible for:
- Agreeing and communicating the aims of the Assessment. (see also preceding Steps 1. and 2.)
- Reviewing and "Signing-Off" the final Submission Document/Self-Assessment package as a valid representation of the organisations performance.
- Agreeing in advance how to analyse and use the Feedback report or Self-Assessment outcomes.
- Provision of needed resources, often the time of themselves and/or others.
- Being available to unblock conflicts on priorities or other road-blocks that may emerge.

Criterion Part Owners (CPO's)

It is a good practice to assign managerial or executive level responsibilities for specific Criterion-parts or groupings. This can help during periods of Award Submission or Self-Assessment but in many high performing organisations such responsibilities are also an on-going part of daily and strategic management.

In an Award Submission (or Self-Assessment) project, Criterion Part Owners (CPO's) should be responsible for:

- Supporting the Submission Document Project Team (see following description) by ensuring that the information for their Criterion-parts is collected, collated and transmitted in a suitable format.
- Supporting/leading specific site visit meetings, i.e. they will be the key interviewees for their assigned Criterion-parts.
- Ensuring that the actions identified as priorities from the Feedback Report, related to their Criterion are implemented.

As part of an on-going daily and strategic management role, a CPO should be responsible for the optimisation of their assigned Criterion-parts. As a way of summarising/testing their role, there are 7 things an effective Criterion-part owner should be able to do/describe:

An effective Criterion Part Owner can describe, for the Criterion-parts they own

1. The rationale behind selecting/continuing to use chosen approaches/processes/measures over others that may be available for their Criterion.
2. How on-going internal and external learning is undertaken to help the organisation better understand ever changing leading global practices and what alternatives may be available.
3. The outcomes being achieved for their Criterion-parts; - the performance over time, both effectiveness and efficiency, in meaningful numerical terms with references to the organisation's targets, the aspirations of involved stakeholders and, where applicable, comparisons with strategically key performance insights from other organisations.
4. A sound logic by which the targets are set related to the owned Criterion-parts -e.g. is the goal setting appropriately based on a use of strategy alignment and/or historical data and/or comparative insights from other organisations and/or stakeholder needs?
5. How extensive, methodical, repeatable and aligned (to other approaches) is the deployment of the chosen methods?
6. What improvements or innovations can be demonstrated that have either occurred, or are planned?
7. Why the organisation is confident that the performance will be sustained into the future and how it knows that what it is doing is effective and efficient.

The approach you take in appointing the Criterion owners will depend on your organisation and the nature and capabilities of your management team. The following table shows some good practice groupings of Criterion-parts.

Example of Grouping and Assignment of Criterion Part Owner roles

Leadership Behaviours (1a-1e in Section 7)	Top Executive
People Management, Motivation and Satisfaction (3a-3e and 7a-7b)	Senior Executive
Strategic Environment/Understanding (2a-2b)	Senior Executive
Strategy Formulation (2c)	Senior Executive
Strategy Deployment (2d)	Senior Executive
Partners (4a)	Senior Executive
Finances (4b)	Senior Executive
Buildings, Equipment, Materials and Natural Resources (4c)	Senior Executive
Knowledge and Technology (4d-4e)	Senior Executive
External Stakeholder Outcomes (5e, 6a-6b, 8a-8b)	Senior Executive
Business Outcomes (9a-9b)	Senior Executive
Process Design, QA and Excellence (5a)	Senior Executive
Marketing (5c)	Senior Executive
Process/Service Design and Realisation (5b, 5d)	Multiple Owners/Function Heads

Note: In a smaller organisation, or as your first step, some of these assignments could be combined, for instance, combining strategy (2a-2d) with Business Outcomes (9a-9b). The Criterion-part references are fully explained in the flow diagrams within Section 7.

Submission (or Self-Assessment) Project Team (SPT)

It is a common and valid practice, in addition to, but not in place of, the assignment of EMT and CPO roles, for a small project team to be given the role of coordinating the creation of the Award Submission Document or Self-Assessment.

It is important, if you are serious about getting a valid assessment, that you use capable and experienced people in this team. It can be a great temporary placement for a fast track manger, enabling them to quickly get perspectives on overall organisational performance. An effective Submission Project Team will contain individuals who are respected throughout the organisation, knowledgeable of the organisation and perhaps lastly, or at formation, least importantly, they will know something about the EFQM Model and be able to "think like an Assessor" (but at the start this is probably the least critical selection factor as training can quickly fix any gaps in knowledge).

Within a Submission Project Team a number of tasks/roles will emerge and these are often assigned to specific team members. A Submission Project Team will typically assign roles to:

- **Gatherers** - Those team members responsible for working with (or maybe are) Criterion Part Owners (see previous section) and identifying sources of knowledge and for collecting and sharing potential inputs to submission documents.
- **Writers** - Those responsible for reviewing information from the Gatherers and producing a first draft submission. Specific Criterion-parts are often assigned to specific team members. Gatherers and Writers can be one and the same.
- **Editor(s)** - An individual, or at the very maximum, two people, tasked to edit together the Criterion documents and producing a readable, well designed, cohesive submission. These will be the individual(s) who will make the decisions on what information to lead with, which examples are best, etc. The editor has the challenge of gluing together the inputs of the Criterion owners/writers. The individual will need the gravitas and presence to ensure this is done with the agreement of the Executive Management Team.
- **Project Leader** - An individual, who may also be the Editor, who has overall team management responsibility.

Step 5

Create a Sound Plan

Clearly timescales and budgets need to be agreed and assigned. The debate is often cyclical, the more resources you have the faster you may be able to proceed, so any examples we give here can clearly be challenged, extended or accelerated, but it is not uncommon for the process of preparing a first Award Submission Document, or equivalent Self-Assessment package, in a large organisation (assuming you want to do it robustly) to involve one person-year's worth of work, spread across the whole team and over a 4+ month window.

Example of Grouping and Assignment of Criterion Part Owner roles

Week 0	Gain commitment to go forward
Week1-2	Kick-Off: Recruit and Prepare the teams
Week 2	Initiate communication programme
Week 3-6	Information Safari: (Initial information gathering/scan/meetings)
Week 7-8	Submission Document Outline: -First simple draft
Week 9	First draft review
Week 10-12	Further information gathering/second draft
Week 13-14	Complete second draft
Week 15	Final review and finishing
Week 16	Final Submission Document signed off by EMT
Week 17-??	Site Visit planning (for Awards) and/or Self-Assessment Workshops
Post Site Visit	Receiving and acting upon Feedback

When creating your own plan detailed consideration should be given to:

Planning your Information Gathering and Sharing (The Information "Safari")

Whether you are making an Award Submission or undertaking an equivalent rigorous Self-Assessment, your first use of the EFQM Excellence Model will often involve you in pulling together/analysing performance and practices in a more holistic way than you may have done before. You will often need to undertake a period of information gathering, scanning, meeting and analysis (an "Information Safari/hunt") to create the basis for the submission/assessment.

The Result and Enabler Mapping Templates in Section 7 are designed to help you understand and assess your performance/data and help you do this. They can form the basis of a robust Self-Assessment whether you choose to use them to help you write an Award Submission Document or not. A realistic amount of time/resource (particularly in year 1 when the "baseline" is formulated) will need to be allocated to this phase if you wish to create a robust submission/assessment.

In terms of elapsed time, the information gathering and subsequent drafting/editing tasks (if you are applying to win an Award) typically need to be iterative steps and although successful exceptions can exist, a three to four month lead time between starting the information collection and completing of an Award Submission Document package is often needed.

When completing the Result and Enabler Mapping templates (Section 7 of this book) keep in mind that sources of performance or process insight should not be limited in any way. Examples of common sources of insight include:

- Management Information - Budgets and forecasts, plans, strategy documents, project reports and such like.
- Process Information - Operating procedures, process performance data and such like
- Previous Submissions/Assessments - Your analysis of any previous Feedback Reports and how you have used them as part of a review cycle, what improvements you have achieved and such like..
- Notice-boards/lobby boards - Often forgotten (and often dated?)
- Meeting Minutes - Excellence is a never ending journey and, there is always a "next step", you need to show how you are reviewing your overall performance and the minutes of key meetings can often be cited to help you to do this.
- Annual Reports and Presentations - You may have past presentations to summarise your organisation's overall achievements.
- Press Coverage - testimonials or positive press coverage (if truly independent/unfunded/unsolicited)

With a broad range of information sources in mind a good first step is for CPOs and Writers to have a planning meeting before they fill in a first draft of the Result and Enabler Mapping templates (Section 7). It can often be useful for an SPT to prepare a high level map to show the Criterion impact of the key approaches /enablers used (and related sources of information). For example creating a map, such as the one following, can facilitate the process of identifying and sharing information before completing the detailed templates in section 7.

Example of high level enabler mapping:

Key Enablers	1a	1b	1c	1d	1e	2a	2b	2c	2d	3a	3b	3c	3d	3e	4a	4b	4c	4d	4e	5a	5b	5c	5d	5e
Develop stakeholder management plan		X																				X		
Review and update strategic (mission, vision and values)	X																							
Identify key priority areas																								
Develop, review and update strategic KPIs								X																
etc								X																

Such a high level map will demonstrate the areas in which gathering information, in more detail, will be beneficial.

Planning to Document your Performance

Whether making an Award Submission Document or doing a Self-Assessment you need to summarise and document your performance evidence. If you are undertaking a Self-Assessment, probably just completing the Enabler and Result Mapping Templates in this book will be enough for you to undertake a robust internal assessment. If you are applying for an Award using an Enabler Map process (EFQM Excellence Award only), you can probably simply transfer from the forms in section 7 to an Enabler Map template prescribed/given by the Award Administration. However if you are using a full Submission Document process you will have the extra challenge/opportunity of creating the 75-page Submission Document with the aim of realistically communicating your current achievements and methods to the Assessors.

Creating Submission(s) is truly both a challenge (it takes time and needs editorial thought) and an opportunity (if done well it will help the Assessors plan an effective site visit and lessen your need for communicating detailed insights to the Assessors when they are on site). It also becomes a great internal and external communication "pack" for on-going, post Assessment, use.

Good practices to keep in mind include:

When Summarising Enabler Practices

The Enablers cover the first five Criteria and focus on how you manage your organisation. When summarising/documenting your performance remember to describe:

- The rationale behind selecting/continuing to use your chosen approaches/processes/measures (for their Criterion-parts) over others that may be available.
- How on-going internal and external learning is undertaken to help your organisation better understand ever changing leading global practices and what alternatives may be available.

- How extensive, methodical, repeatable and aligned (to other approaches) is the deployment of your chosen methods. If a change is only part way through its implementation, ensure this is made clear to the Assessors by describing where, in the deployment process, you are.
- Some "history" and context; -how did the methods you have now evolve as innovations/ improvements from refinement of previous approaches, how will they evolve and refine in line with the strategic challenges you described when concluding the Key Information that will frame the assessment (see Step 3).

When Summarising Results Performance:

The Results cover the last four Criteria and focus on what you have achieved in your organisation and how that compares to others. When summarising/documenting your results performance remember to describe:

- The outcomes being achieved for each Criterion-part; - the performance over time, both effectiveness and efficiency, in meaningful numerical terms with references to your own organisation's targets, the aspirations of involved stakeholders and, where applicable, comparisons with strategically key performance insights from other organisations.
- A sound logic by which the targets are set -e.g. is the goal setting appropriately based on a use of strategy alignment and/or historical data and/or comparative insights from other organisations and/ or stakeholder needs.
- How you have confidence that the performance will be sustained into the future and how you know that what you are doing is effective and efficient.
- Which results you regard as most key.
- The validity (for the Results stakeholders), of the timeliness, accuracy and reliability of what you measure.
- Context which should be given to explain any variances or negative trends (e.g. "although in a downturn, we are dropping our share slower than our competitors", or "The capital reserve dropped when we invested in the new site")

Dealing with omissions: -If you do not have data, if you do not have approaches, if you have no comparison data, then you will need to communicate these omissions in context. All organisations are on a journey (Sustainable Excellence is a never ending race) and you should show how the omissions are likely to be resolved by your future plans. The Submission Document should represent how you operate and manage your organisation at the time of writing, but with you future challenges and opportunities in mind.

Planning - Document Production Standards

You will need to create some basic production, document control and style standards, these will often need to follow specific rules set by your Award Administrator and will cover areas such as:

- Use of **covers and dividers**
- **Page Layout** - What page structure will you use? (for readability and use of space, two columns is commonly regarded as efficient). What are your typeface and paragraph rules?
- **Page Allocations** - What is your target length for each Criterion response? Perhaps weighted by the points available? Do you have a page limit to work to (often, in a full submission, x75 pages, A4)?
- **Cross-referencing plans** - Some methods/data you will probably only list or describe once, for example the existence of a Scorecard approach may be introduced and fully described in 2c and 2d, but will be referred back to from other Criterion.
- Standards for **consistency with Diagrams and Graphs**.
- **Grammatical format** - How you will refer to your organisation? Will you use the "first person" or other format when referring to "your" organisation e.g. "After reviewing our strategy, we put in place additional research to help us develop the "XYZ" products for the Indian market place"
- **Glossary of Terms** - Consider creating a "Glossary of Terms" if you are acronym bound (and if you are not, please e-mail we are looking for a role model!).
- **Document control** - To ensure that your progress, over what is often a time window of several weeks of drafting, can be effectively shared, you will need to establish mechanisms enabling multiple access, traceability and version control.

Success Factors:

If you are documenting, well, your performance into an effective Submission Document it will have the following characteristics:

1. It will show the organisation in an honest but positive way, you will feel proud when you read it.
2. It will recognise that Excellence is a never-ending journey and show the next steps that exist for you.
3. It will tell the story of the organisation, to some degree the past but most importantly your present and future (your readiness for the challenges and opportunities of tomorrow).
4. It will be written with the Assessor team in mind.

Planning for the Site Visit (or if you are Self-Assessing your Assessment day)

In an Award process, it can be said that the purpose of the Submission Document is primarily to enable the Assessor team to plan a site visit. No matter how comprehensive the Submission Documents are the impressions formed by the Assessor during the site visit will be key and you need to ensure you plan well for a site visit and have easy and timely access to your supportive data sets and evidence during the visit. A key to a successful site visit is preparation and ensuring that everyone likely to be visited is ready to openly and honestly answer whatever questions may arise.

You will likely be in extensive dialogue with your Assessment Team Leader to plan the visit and will probably get some (but limited) insights to begin to understand what the team wishes to learn during the visit.

However, equally, maybe even more importantly, you can form your own views on the key points a team may wish to verify/clarify by having someone independent from the Submission Writers Team, assess the Submission Documents you produced, (Apply the full EFQM process and RADAR), before the Assessor team arrives, in order to conclude what may be likely Site Visit Subjects that will arise during your assessment. This "independent" person can come from within your own organisation or another. They would need to have practical experience of being an Assessor, i.e. not just passing the EFQM Assessor Training Course. EFQM holds a register of individuals who have attended and passed the International Assessor Training Course and you could consult this Directory if you feel a truly "external" view would be helpful.

Whether you do a pre-assessment or not, all key managers should prepare by reading the Submission Document in a depth appropriate to their role. The visiting Assessors will want to see the information used to manage the organisation on a daily basis and will be influenced by how responsive the interviewees are. A good practice preparation process is to carry out "rehearsal interviews" and establish what communication gaps can be filled before site visit.

In the days immediately prior to the visit/assessment, it is wise to review/address any "housekeeping" issues; -Are all notice boards up to date with relevant information? Is the reception area tidy? Are all the logistics (for the Assessors) planned and ready to be managed? If you are offering translators (if needed) or guides to the team, have they been appropriately briefed? Have you established a feedback process so that Assessor hosts/ guides and the interviewees can provide information on what has been covered and common themes can then be communicated to subsequent interviewees?

Step 6

Spot and Overcome Typical Road-Blocks (Manage your Plan)

Progress on your assessment project should be regularly reviewed and certainly added to the agenda of all key management meetings in the typically 3-4+ month window in which a Submission Document is prepared. Common pitfalls to watch for include:

Lack of consensus on the key messages to be communicated in a Submission Document or Self-Assessment.

There are always decisions to make on what information to lead with, which examples are best, etc. To help get a consensus on the editorial "glue" to use to hold together an Assessment Submission, it can be useful to get the Executive Management Team to take the Elevator Test...

- Ask each member of the team to write down "What would we say if we had 60 seconds (time between floors in an elevator) to describe the five or six points that best characterise the Strengths of our organisation?"
- Debate this with the whole group to attempt to achieve a consensus.
- Use the outcome to ensure the agreed points are brought out in the responses to each Criterion in the Submission Document and are kept in mind during the site visit.

Be careful with managing consultants if you use them.

Around the world there are many examples of both good and bad practice with using consultants as part of the Submission Document team/process. Used well, a consultant can help you by providing expert knowledge of the EFQM Model and process, and releasing time within the organisation. They also bring an external, independent view and are not hampered by the internal politics or other distractions.

Assuming you are not so foolish as to think that you will get any value from having a consultant trying to fool the Assessors by making up an Application that may "win" (but does not honestly reflect reality in your organisation), then the key risks to manage are those related to loss of control and the time needed for them to fully understand your organisation.

Loss of control jeopardises the engagement/ownership of the Assessment process by the organisation's managers and employees. These stakeholders can become one, or more, steps removed from the reality of the Assessment and will not be best prepared to receive and act on the Assessment outcomes. Appropriate project management of consultants with clear review processes (that involve all key stakeholders) can help overcome this risk.

If a consultant does not fully understand your business you increase the risk of an outcome being either the (costly) production of a document that does not best describe your organisation and its achievements, or a need for an enormous amount of time to be given to briefing the consultant. Time invested in finding a consultant who understands your sector/business can be time well spent.

Step 7

Preparing for and using the Feedback Report
(or acting on the outcomes of your Self-Assessment)

Prior to receiving a Feedback Report or Assessment outcome, particularly in your first assessment, it is vital that you prepare your managers to ensure they are not shocked by what they receive. Expectations may need to be managed and good practices include ensuring that all involved are aware that:

- The analysis process is limited by the team understanding of your achievements and methods. –If you (or they) did not communicate, realistically and well (particularly during the site visit), your successes will not have been fully understood and you will not receive a complete analysis.
- If you are entering for an Award that replicates exactly the EFQM Excellence Award process then be aware that the precision of scoring is to within 10% score bands at the Criterion/Criterion part level and in overall points/1000 (see also Section 7), you will not receive an absolute number but rather a positioning within a 50-point band.
- The Strengths and Areas for Improvement you will receive are driven out of the assessment of your performance against the EFQM Excellence Model. This is invariably perceived to be very useful, but the comments are not ranked according to your strategic priorities. This is a task you need to plan to do yourselves.
- There can be up to 250 Areas for Improvement. Most organisations do not plan to address all of them in the short term.

In a high performing organisation, the management team will be eagerly anticipating the feedback with the aim of using the performance insights arising from the Award Assessment/Application to actively drive improvements in the organisation.

Once you have received your Feedback Report a good next step is to use a systematic approach to prioritisation and action planning. A very simple but effective way of reviewing and acting on an Award Feedback Report or the outcome of a Self-Assessment can be to follow the 5 step Ease-Impact review:

Ease and Impact 5 Step Analysis

1 **Group and Merge Common Issues** - Take the, say, 150-250 Areas for Improvement from the Criterion-part level analysis and thematically group them, for example many Areas for Improvement in Criterion 3 and 7 may be actionable by acting on a small number of people focussed projects. Post-It (yellow sticky notes) based "affinity diagrams" are one technique that can help with this. *This may reduce the number to say 50-75 thematically grouped opportunities, but, at this stage do not "throw anything out".*

2 **Review the Strengths** - Add into the list any actions relating to any potential projects related to Strengths that you want to reinforce. *You may have now 60-80 opportunities.*

3 **Strategically Prioritise the "Impact" of each** - Assess strategic impact of each of the 60-80 on some simple scale from 'low' to 'medium' to 'high' impact.

Assess Potential Project: IMPACT		
Low (0 points)	Medium (3 points)	High (5 points)
Is unlikely to significantly impact any of our strategic performance goals	Has some impact on one or more of our strategic performance goals	Has significant impact on several strategic performance goals

4 **Assess the "Ease" of acting on each** - Assign some simple evaluation scale, which can summarise the ease by which each potential action/project could be accomplished in terms of Investment in time, money or effort. Be clear on the timescale for this assessment, for example:

Assess Potential Project: EASE		
Hard (0 points)	Medium (3 points)	Easy (5 points)
• Unlikely to be achieved within 6-9 months • Will require significant resources • Is dependent on factors external to the organisation or department	• Likely to be implemented within 6-9 months • Will require a reasonable amount of resources • Is not highly dependent on factors external to the organisation or department	• Can be implemented in relevant timescales • Resources are not a limiting factor • Is within the control of our organisation, or department, external dependencies are manageable or do not exist

5 **Create a ranking table and/or an X-Y grid to help make your final decisions** - Probably a mix of data and intuition will now help you come to some conclusions on what to act on. A simple prioritisation table can help:

i.Possible Project	ii.Impact on Business Goals (0-5)	iii.Ease to Deliver (in 9 or? m.)	iv.Ranking Score (ii. x iii.)	v.Ranked Order
Implemented X	5	3	15	1
Initiate Y	3	3	9	2

However strategic improvement is often about managing a portfolio of projects/actions. Plotting the outcomes of your Ease and Impact categorisations in a matrix grid can help you to select a balanced portfolio of projects. For example:

Ease-Impact Matrix

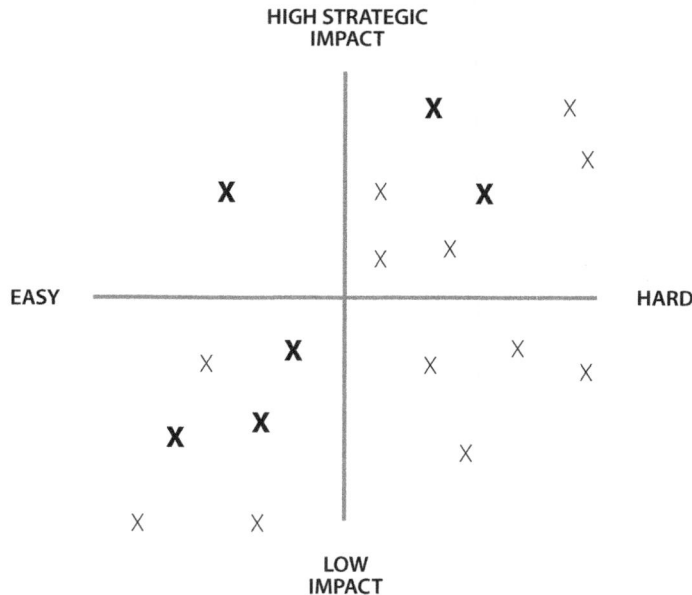

HIGH STRATEGIC IMPACT

EASY — HARD

LOW IMPACT

Mapping potential projects in this way enables selection decisions to be easily debated. In reality, after taking the easy decisions this often results into debating which project to select in a line of mapped potential projects starting in the bottom left quadrant and leading to the top right (the emboldened examples in the diagram). Most organisations choose a balanced portfolio of some quick, but valid, wins (bottom left, easy to do but not the highest impact) along with an essential but limited number of bigger but more beneficial challenges (in the top right, harder to do but highly beneficial).

The most easy decisions to take are of course if your analysis puts a project in the bottom right quadrant. - Then you would be unwise to plan to act on the "expensive trivia" (low impact, hard to do) and you will of course have quickly decided to act on anything that falls into the top left quadrant (easy to do, high impact, "no brainers").

7. Enabler and Result Mapping Templates
(to help you prepare your Submission Document or perform a Self-Assessment).

How to use the pro-forma templates

The following pages contain a series of analysis templates to help you either Self-Assess your performance and/or prepare to make an Award Submission Document.

We suggest you assign the completion of specific templates to members of a Self-Assessment or Submission Document creation team, have them do some preparatory work, and then, as a management or project team, come back together to draw your final conclusions.

In the following pages each pro-forma leads you through a self-explanatory series of steps to analyse your performance against each Criterion. At the beginning of each there is a diagram to help you understand what to assess, followed by a number of good practice insights to help you learn what leaders in excellent organisations do for the Criterion-part that you are analysing.

For a full analysis of the Enablers, complete steps 1 through to 4 on each pro-forma and then score your analysis. The steps to follow, for Enablers, (also listed on each pro-forma) are:

Step 1   Understand what to Assess (Review the EFQM Model)
Step 2   Summarise your management methods that impact on the Criterion or Criterion parts
            (See *Note below), this includes:
                2.1 Mapping your Enablers
                2.2 Summarising Deployment
                2.3 Listing Reviews and Refinements
Step 3   Review the good practices of others
Step 4   Conclude your views on Strengths and Areas for Improvement
Step 5   Produce a RADAR estimate for the analysis

*Note: If you are preparing an Award Submission Document you should additionally:

1. Segment the analysis by Criterion-parts, e.g. in Leadership 1a to 1e as per the flow diagram for the Criterion, if this is the preferred format for you Award application.

2. Consider stopping at Step 2, as this provides you the source material for your drafting of the Award Submission Documents, and scoring/analysis may be best done after the completion of, and based on, the Submission Documents you create

For each Result Criterion, complete a set of slightly different steps 1 to 4 and then score your analysis. The steps to follow, for Results, (also listed on each pro-forma) are:

Step 1   Understand what to Assess (Review the EFQM Model)
Step 2   Create a data review summary for the Criterion *(See * note on the previous page)*, this includes:
        2.1 Listing the measures you have and use
        2.2 Analysing your trends over three years (more if available)
        2.3 Reviewing your performance to your targets
        2.4 Comparing your performance to others
        2.5 Listing related Enablers
Step 3   Review the good practices of others for the Criterion
Step 4   Conclude your views on Strengths and Areas for Improvement
Step 5   Produce a RADAR estimate for the analysis

When you have completed the templates you will have a comprehensive summary of your current performance in the framework of the EFQM Excellence Model. This summary can then be used to either inform your Self-Assessment of your performance and/or aid the creation of Award Submission Documents by forming a key input for the drafting team.

Using the RADAR Quick-Score tools on the pro-forma templates

To fully apply RADAR to the level used by Award Assessors typically necessitates three or more days of extensive training and does not make the approach accessible to many (certainly Senior) managers.

The Quick-Score RADAR estimate tools (on each pro-forma template) are simplifications of EFQM's RADAR Assessment methodology designed for, and proven to be, useable without the need for extensive training.

These Quick-Score estimate tools are not intended to compete with or replace the full EFQM RADAR approach, as used by Award Assessors and those wishing to fully apply RADAR with the same rigour/precision as Award Assessors should also consider attending an EFQM International Assessor Training Programme.

The tools on each pro-forma set are self-explanatory but readers with no prior experience of RADAR may like to note that RADAR is a key component of the EFQM Excellence Model, and is the tool used by most Award Assessors to assign numbers to their analysis.

The RADAR acronym consists of four groups of key words:

Results,
Approach,
Deployment,
Assessment and **R**efinement

This logic behind RADAR, is that to be sustainably excellent an organisation needs to; -

- Determine the Results it is aiming for as part of its strategic process.
- Plan and develop an integrated set of sound Approaches to deliver the required Results both now and in the future.
- Deploy the approaches in a systematic way to ensure full implementation.
- Assess and Refine the approaches used based on monitoring and analysis of the Results achieved and on-going learning activities which will lead to a review of performance and implementation of refinements, with global good practice in mind.

Note also that the RADAR technique is often used as part of daily management in mature organisation/users of the Model.

Enabler and Result Mapping Templates

Step 1 Understanding the EFQM Model

Excellent organisations have leaders who shape the future and make it happen, acting as role models for its values and ethics and inspiring trust at all times. They are flexible, enabling the organisation to anticipate and react in a timely manner to ensure the on-going success of the organisation.

They assess their performance and manage the five critical areas shown in the Criterion-parts on the right.

Defining what's expected

Putting in place processess to get there

Engaging external parties

1a Set **Mission, Vision, Values, Ethics, Role Models**

1b Develop & Implement **Management Systems**

1c Interact with **External Stakeholders**

1e Maintain a flexible organisation & **Champion Change**

1d Communicate, movivate and reinforce a **Culture of Excellence**

Setting the tempo

Reinforcing behaviour

Step 2 Summarise your management methods and how they impact on the Leadership Criterion

2.1 Map your Enablers List/map the processes and approaches (groups of processes) that you have that impact on these Criterion parts	2.2 Summarise Deployment Log to what extent do you intend to deploy each approach and how you can demonstrate you've done it?	2.3 List Reviews and Refinements Log how often you review these approaches and the overall mix of approaches? What refinements have been made?

2.1 Map your Enablers	2.2 Summarise Deployment	2.3 List Reviews and Refinements
List/map the processes and approaches (groups of processes) that you have that impact on these Criterion parts	Log to what extent do you intend to deploy each approach and how you can demonstrate you've done it?	Log how often you review these approaches and the overall mix of approaches? What refinements have been made?

Step 3 Review the good practices of others

Our experience with Award winners leads us to conclude that the following are generically good practices. You may find these useful to review, along with your own organisational specific research and learning on good practice approaches, before you conclude your analysis of Strengths and Areas for Improvement for this Criterion.

In our experience Leaders in high performing organisations put emphasis on:

1 Showing that they "Know what they expect" and ensure everyone "knows how they will realise it".
2 Personally meeting with, and knowing the needs and expectations of, their key stakeholders.
3 Respecting, understanding and transparently engaging with people at all levels in the organisation and its Key Partners, Alliances, Customers and Suppliers.
4 Stimulating and participating in innovative and creative thinking by personally using the improvement methodologies provided for their people, thereby role modelling desired behaviours.
5 Understanding how their leadership behaviour influences others and using fact-based processes to obtain feedback on their personal and collective leadership behaviour.
6 Understanding what motivates and de-motivates their people and teams and aligning their reward and recognition processes with such expectations in mind.
7 Creating transparent, efficient and effective governance and management systems, ensuring that clear roles and accountabilities are assigned.
8 Maintaining foresight of a range of change scenarios, both positive and negative, that may affect the organisation and building awareness in their people and other stakeholders of the likely changes needed were these to occur.
9 Ensuring that people act with integrity and values and confront any variances.
10 Coaching and supporting other leaders at all levels.

From my own experiences I would also include an emphasis on:

List your own research in your sector/organisation

Step 4 Conclude an analysis of your key Strengths and Areas for Improvement for this Criterion

Strengths	Areas for Improvement

RADAR Estimate for Leadership Criterion

Decision 1: Quick score the Approaches used in this Criterion

We don't manage this very formally.	We know what we need to do; some structured approaches are now in place.	Relevant, *soundly based* approaches in place, in many areas.	Proven, sound, refined, well *integrated* approaches in most areas.	Approaches can be shown to be at world-class role model levels.

0	1	2	3	4	5	6	7	8	9	10	11	12	13	14	15	16	17	18	19	20	21	22	23	24	25	26	27	28	29	30	31	32	33

Keep in mind your summary of +/-'s and tick a single number above, remember that:

- *Soundly based:* means the approaches have clear rationales, defined processes and focus on stakeholder needs.
- *Integrated:* means that the approaches support policy and strategy and are linked to other approaches where appropriate.

Decision 2: Quick score Deployment of the approaches used in this Criterion

We've not deployed our ideas in a structured way.	The approaches are *implemented* to less than 25% of their intended potential.	We can show evidence of *implementation* to 50% of the full potential.	Clear and *Systematic implementation* to 75% of full potential across all areas.	Our approaches are robustly *implemented* to full potential in all relevant areas.

0	1	2	3	4	5	6	7	8	9	10	11	12	13	14	15	16	17	18	19	20	21	22	23	24	25	26	27	28	29	30	31	32	33

Keep in mind your summary of +/-'s and tick a single number above, remember that:

- *Implemented:* means the extent to which the approach is put into effective use/deployment.
- *Systematic:* means that as well as being deployed, you judge that the deployment was carried out in a structured way with the method used to ensure deployment being itself planned and executed soundly.

Decision 3: Quick score the Assessment and Refinement of this Criterion

We do not do assess and refine in a structured way.	Occasional measurement and review of the approaches used in the Criterion.	Good evidence of measurement, review, learning from others and improvement.	Regular, effective measurement and process level learning is undertaken. Creativity, innovation & improvement is evident.	All approaches are regularly refined, learning and innovation can be comprehensively demonstrated.

0	1	2	3	4	5	6	7	8	9	10	11	12	13	14	15	16	17	18	19	20	21	22	23	24	25	26	27	28	29	30	31	32	33

Keep in mind your summary of +/-'s and tick a single number above, remember that:

- *Measurement:* means the extent to which regular and appropriate measurement of the effectiveness and efficiency of the approach and its deployment takes place.
- *Learning:* has a scope that includes the extent to which knowledge transfer takes place to identify good practice focussed improvement opportunities and how creativity is used to stimulate ideas.
- *Improvement:* means the extent to which the output from measurement and learning is analysed and used in order to identify, prioritise, plan and implement improvements and innovations.

RADAR percentage - quick score prediction for this Criterion:

Decision 1 Approach Score	Decision 2 Deployment Score	Decision 3 Refinement Score	Predicted Overall %
			_____ % (=Total of Decision 1+2+3)

Step 1 Understanding the EFQM Model

Excellent Organisations implement their Mission and Vision by developing a stakeholder focused strategy.

Policies, plans, objectives and processes are developed and deployed to deliver the strategy.

They assess and mange the four critical areas shown in the Criterion-parts opposite.

2a Needs & expectations of **both Stakeholders and the external environment**

2b Understanding of **Internal performance and capabilities**

Inputs

2c Develop, Review & Update Strategy

Strategy Development

2d Communicate, **Implement and Monitor Strategy and Policy**

Policy Deployment

Step 2 Summarise your management methods and how they impact on the Strategy Criterion

2.1 Map your Enablers	2.2 Summarise Deployment	2.3 List Reviews and Refinements
List/map the processes and approaches (groups of processes) that you have that impact on these Criterion parts	Log to what extent do you intend to deploy each approach and how you can demonstrate you've done it?	Log how often you review these approaches and the overall mix of approaches? What refinements have been made?

2.1 Map your Enablers	2.2 Summarise Deployment	2.3 List Reviews and Refinements
List/map the processes and approaches (groups of processes) that you have that impact on these Criterion parts	Log to what extent do you intend to deploy each approach and how you can demonstrate you've done it?	Log how often you review these approaches and the overall mix of approaches? What refinements have been made?

Step 3 Review the good practices of others

Our experience with Award winners leads us to conclude that the following are generically good practices. You may find these useful to review, along with your own organisational specific research and learning on good practice approaches before you conclude your analysis of Strengths and Areas for Improvement for this Criterion.

In our analyses we find that high performing organisations are:

1   Effective at acquiring, analysing, and widely disseminating reliable stakeholder and market focused information and anticipating the impact of potential conflicts resulting from their attempted balancing of the needs and priorities of different stakeholders.

2   Tracking the competitive, environmental, societal, economic, and demographic factors, which may change stakeholder behaviour and create opportunity or risk.

3   Creating a range of future scenarios to sensitise managers to potential opportunities/risks and help strategic planning.

4   Understanding their current performance/competences and which future core business competencies will likely enable success in the scenarios they foresee.

5   Maintaining a framework of key processes to deliver strategy and develop needed competencies.

6   Realising that strategic and operational speed may be important and using cycle time as a driver so rapid deployment can occur.

7   Strategically reviewing past achievements, or failures, and attempting to understand causality.

8   Predicting what are the key results that will most likely drive their future success and managing them closely.

9   Communicating strategies, policies and plans to key stakeholders, monitoring their performance and listening to their feedback.

10 Operating plans, budgets and performance review and reward processes that recognises strategically relevant outcomes and efforts.

From my own experiences I would also include an emphasis on:

List your own research in your sector/organisation

Step 4 Conclude an analysis of your key Strengths and Areas for Improvement for this Criterion

Strengths	Areas for Improvement

Decision 1: Quick score the Approaches used in this Criterion

We don't manage this very formally.	We know what we need to do; some structured approaches are now in place.	Relevant, *soundly based* approaches in place, in many areas.	Proven, sound, refined, well *integrated* approaches in most areas.	Approaches can be shown to be at world-class role model levels.

0	1	2	3	4	5	6	7	8	9	10	11	12	13	14	15	16	17	18	19	20	21	22	23	24	25	26	27	28	29	30	31	32	33

Keep in mind your summary of +/-'s and tick a single number above, remember that:

- *Soundly based:* means the approaches have clear rationales, defined processes and focus on stakeholder needs.
- *Integrated:* means that the approaches support policy and strategy and are linked to other approaches where appropriate.

Decision 2: Quick score Deployment of the approaches used in this Criterion

We've not deployed our ideas in a structured way.	The approaches are *implemented* to less than 25% of their intended potential.	We can show evidence of *implementation* to 50% of the full potential.	Clear and *Systematic implementation* to 75% of full potential across all areas.	Our approaches are robustly *implemented* to full potential in all relevant areas.

0	1	2	3	4	5	6	7	8	9	10	11	12	13	14	15	16	17	18	19	20	21	22	23	24	25	26	27	28	29	30	31	32	33

Keep in mind your summary of +/-'s and tick a single number above, remember that:

- *Implemented:* means the extent to which the approach is put into effective use/deployment.
- *Systematic:* means that as well as being deployed, you judge that the deployment was carried out in a structured way with the method used to ensure deployment being itself planned and executed soundly.

Decision 3: Quick score the **Assessment and Refinement** of this Criterion				
We do not do assess and refine in a structured way.	Occasional measurement and review of the approaches used in the Criterion.	Good evidence of measurement, review, learning from others and improvement.	Regular, effective measurement and process level learning is undertaken. Creativity, innovation & improvement is evident.	All approaches are regularly refined, learning and innovation can be comprehensively demonstrated.

0	1	2	3	4	5	6	7	8	9	10	11	12	13	14	15	16	17	18	19	20	21	22	23	24	25	26	27	28	29	30	31	32	33

Keep in mind your summary of +/-'s and tick a single number above, remember that:

- *Measurement:* means the extent to which regular and appropriate measurement of the effectiveness and efficiency of the approach and its deployment takes place.
- *Learning:* has a scope that includes the extent to which knowledge transfer takes place to identify good practice focussed improvement opportunities and how creativity is used to stimulate ideas.
- *Improvement:* means the extent to which the output from measurement and learning is analysed and used in order to identify, prioritise, plan and implement improvements and innovations.

RADAR percentage - quick score prediction for this Criterion:

Decision 1 Approach Score	**Decision 2** Deployment Score	**Decision 3** Refinement Score	**Predicted Overall %**
			_____ % (=Total of Decision 1+2+3)

Step 1 Understanding the EFQM Model

Excellent organisations value their people and create a culture that allows the mutually beneficial achievement of organisational and personal goals. They develop the capabilities of their people and promote fairness and equality. They care for, communicate, reward and recognise, in a way that motivates people, builds commitment and enables them to use their skills and knowledge for the benefit of the organisation.

They assess their performance and manage the five critical areas shown opposite.

3a People plans **Alignment to strategy**

3e Reward, Recognition & Care

3b Knowledge & Capabilities are developed

3c Alignment, Involvement & Empowerment

Positive Environment

Capability focused on objectives

Action

3d Effective Communication at all levels

Step 2 Summarise your management methods and how they impact on the People Criterion

2.1 Map your Enablers List/map the processes and approaches (groups of processes) that you have that impact on these Criterion parts	2.2 Summarise Deployment Log to what extent do you intend to deploy each approach and how you can demonstrate you've done it?	2.3 List Reviews and Refinements Log how often you review these approaches and the overall mix of approaches? What refinements have been made?

2.1 Map your Enablers	2.2 Summarise Deployment	2.3 List Reviews and Refinements
List/map the processes and approaches (groups of processes) that you have that impact on these Criterion parts	Log to what extent do you intend to deploy each approach and how you can demonstrate you've done it?	Log how often you review these approaches and the overall mix of approaches? What refinements have been made?

Step 3 Review the good practices of others

Our experience with Award winners leads us to conclude that the following are generically good practices. You may find these useful to review, along with your own organisational specific research and learning on good practice approaches before you conclude your analysis of Strengths and Areas for Improvement for this Criterion.

In our analyses we find that high performing organisations put emphasis on:

1. Developing people numbers and capabilities consistent with strategy and policy to meet current, emerging and future business needs.
2. Ensuring organisational structures are aligned with key processes, and that clarity of people roles and accountabilities exists within the structure.
3. Ensuring that team and individual reward/recognition is aligned with cascaded strategic goals.
4. Being willing to confront non-performance, initially with supportive coaching and counselling.
5. Having clarity on the degree of empowerment that they believe is appropriate and making this clear with guidance and clear boundaries.
6. Having robust succession plans for key posts.
7. Systematically identifying the communication expectations of different parts of the organisation and implementing structured plans to manage or satisfy these expectations.
8. Using surveys and other forms of employee feedback/monitoring to get insights on employee's satisfaction and motivation.
9. Understand the contribution of people to the organisation's success, their needs and expectations and how best to be able to care for them.
10. Creating a culture where creativity and innovation is valued, improvement is the norm, and competent failure can be accepted.

From my own experiences I would also include an emphasis on:

List your own research in your sector/organisation

Step 4 Conclude an analysis of your key Strengths and Areas for Improvement for this Criterion

Strengths	Areas for Improvement

RADAR Estimate for People Criterion

Decision 1: Quick score the Approaches used in this Criterion

We don't manage this very formally.	We know what we need to do; some structured approaches are now in place.	Relevant, *soundly based* approaches in place, in many areas.	Proven, sound, refined, well *integrated* approaches in most areas.	Approaches can be shown to be at world-class role model levels.

0	1	2	3	4	5	6	7	8	9	10	11	12	13	14	15	16	17	18	19	20	21	22	23	24	25	26	27	28	29	30	31	32	33

Keep in mind your summary of +/-'s and tick a single number above, remember that:

- *Soundly based:* means the approaches have clear rationales, defined processes and focus on stakeholder needs.
- *Integrated:* means that the approaches support policy and strategy and are linked to other approaches where appropriate.

Decision 2: Quick score Deployment of the approaches used in this Criterion

We've not deployed our ideas in a structured way.	The approaches are *implemented* to less than 25% of their intended potential.	We can show evidence of *implementation* to 50% of the full potential.	Clear and *Systematic implementation* to 75% of full potential across all areas.	Our approaches are robustly *implemented* to full potential in all relevant areas.

0	1	2	3	4	5	6	7	8	9	10	11	12	13	14	15	16	17	18	19	20	21	22	23	24	25	26	27	28	29	30	31	32	33

Keep in mind your summary of +/-'s and tick a single number above, remember that:

- *Implemented:* means the extent to which the approach is put into effective use/deployment.
- *Systematic:* means that as well as being deployed, you judge that the deployment was carried out in a structured way with the method used to ensure deployment being itself planned and executed soundly.

Decision 3: Quick score the Assessment and Refinement of this Criterion

We do not do assess and refine in a structured way.	Occasional measurement and review of the approaches used in the Criterion.	Good evidence of measurement, review, learning from others and improvement.	Regular, effective measurement and process level learning is undertaken. Creativity, innovation & improvement is evident.	All approaches are regularly refined, learning and innovation can be comprehensively demonstrated.

0	1	2	3	4	5	6	7	8	9	10	11	12	13	14	15	16	17	18	19	20	21	22	23	24	25	26	27	28	29	30	31	32	33

Keep in mind your summary of +/-'s and tick a single number above, remember that:

- *Measurement:* means the extent to which regular and appropriate measurement of the effectiveness and efficiency of the approach and its deployment takes place.
- *Learning:* has a scope that includes the extent to which knowledge transfer takes place to identify good practice focussed improvement opportunities and how creativity is used to stimulate ideas.
- *Improvement:* means the extent to which the output from measurement and learning is analysed and used in order to identify, prioritise, plan and implement improvements and innovations.

RADAR percentage - quick score prediction for this Criterion:

Decision 1 Approach Score	**Decision 2** Deployment Score	**Decision 3** Refinement Score	**Predicted Overall** %
			_____ % (=Total of Decision 1+2+3)

Step 1 Understanding the EFQM Model

Excellent organisations plan and manage external partnerships, suppliers and internal resources in order to support strategy and policies and the effective operation of processes. They ensure that that they effectively manage their environmental and societal impact.

They assess their performance and manage the five critical areas shown in the Criterion-parts on the right.

4a Partners and Suppliers	Alignment ⟷
4b Finances	Alignment ⟷
4c Buildings, equipment, materials and natural resources	Alignment ⟷
4d Technology	Alignment ⟷
4e Information & Knowledge	Alignment ⟷

Criterion 2 Strategy

Step 2 Summarise your management methods and how they impact on the Partnership and Resources Criterion

2.1 Map your Enablers List/map the processes and approaches (groups of processes) that you have that impact on these Criterion parts	2.2 Summarise Deployment Log to what extent do you intend to deploy each approach and how you can demonstrate you've done it?	2.3 List Reviews and Refinements Log how often you review these approaches and the overall mix of approaches? What refinements have been made?

2.1 Map your Enablers	2.2 Summarise Deployment	2.3 List Reviews and Refinements
List/map the processes and approaches (groups of processes) that you have that impact on these Criterion parts	Log to what extent do you intend to deploy each approach and how you can demonstrate you've done it?	Log how often you review these approaches and the overall mix of approaches? What refinements have been made?

Step 3 Review the good practices of others

Our experience with Award winners leads us to conclude that the following are generically good practices. You may find these useful to review, along with your own organisational specific research and learning on good practice approaches, before you conclude your analysis of Strengths and Areas for Improvement for this Criterion.

In our analyses we find that high performing organisations put emphasis on:

1   Conducting regular measurement and systematic reviews of the relationships with key partners, including the potential use of the expertise of suppliers and partners in the design of new products and services.
2   Understanding the financing needs for both current and multiple future strategies.
3   Understanding the external controls on financial flexibility that are needed to demonstrate ethical and transparent governance but with maximum freedom to operate within the organisation.
4   Monitoring and managing improvement of financial systems.
5   Maintaining building, materials and equipment strategies linked to future strategic growth needs.
6   Regularly reviewing the use of materials, work in progress and inventory.
7   Tracking and evaluating trends in technology and knowledge and have appropriately robust processes to manage the intellectual property of their own processes and knowledge.
8   Having a strategy for managing knowledge.
9   Operating processes to ensure that information validity, availability, integrity and security / confidentiality are assured.
10 Assessing and developing the environmental performance of the organisation and its suppliers.

From my own experiences I would also include an emphasis on:
List your own research in your sector/organisation

Step 4 Conclude an analysis of your key Strengths and Areas for Improvement for this Criterion

Strengths	Areas for Improvement

RADAR Estimate for
Partnership and Resources Criterion

Decision 1: Quick score the Approaches used in this Criterion

We don't manage this very formally.	We know what we need to do; some structured approaches are now in place.	Relevant, *soundly based* approaches in place, in many areas.	Proven, sound, refined, well *integrated* approaches in most areas.	Approaches can be shown to be at world-class role model levels.

0	1	2	3	4	5	6	7	8	9	10	11	12	13	14	15	16	17	18	19	20	21	22	23	24	25	26	27	28	29	30	31	32	33

Keep in mind your summary of +/-'s and tick a single number above, remember that:

- *Soundly based:* means the approaches have clear rationales, defined processes and focus on stakeholder needs.
- *Integrated:* means that the approaches support policy and strategy and are linked to other approaches where appropriate.

Decision 2: Quick score Deployment of the approaches used in this Criterion

We've not deployed our ideas in a structured way.	The approaches are *implemented* to less than 25% of their intended potential.	We can show evidence of *implementation* to 50% of the full potential.	Clear and *Systematic implementation* to 75% of full potential across all areas.	Our approaches are robustly *implemented* to full potential in all relevant areas.

0	1	2	3	4	5	6	7	8	9	10	11	12	13	14	15	16	17	18	19	20	21	22	23	24	25	26	27	28	29	30	31	32	33

Keep in mind your summary of +/-'s and tick a single number above, remember that:

- *Implemented:* means the extent to which the approach is put into effective use/deployment.
- *Systematic:* means that as well as being deployed, you judge that the deployment was carried out in a structured way with the method used to ensure deployment being itself planned and executed soundly.

Decision 3: Quick score the Assessment and Refinement of this Criterion

We do not do assess and refine in a structured way.	Occasional measurement and review of the approaches used in the Criterion.	Good evidence of measurement, review, learning from others and improvement.	Regular, effective measurement and process level learning is undertaken. Creativity, innovation & improvement is evident.	All approaches are regularly refined, learning and innovation can be comprehensively demonstrated.

0	1	2	3	4	5	6	7	8	9	10	11	12	13	14	15	16	17	18	19	20	21	22	23	24	25	26	27	28	29	30	31	32	33

Keep in mind your summary of +/-'s and tick a single number above, remember that:

- *Measurement:* means the extent to which regular and appropriate measurement of the effectiveness and efficiency of the approach and its deployment takes place.
- *Learning:* has a scope that includes the extent to which knowledge transfer takes place to identify good practice focussed improvement opportunities and how creativity is used to stimulate ideas.
- *Improvement:* means the extent to which the output from measurement and learning is analysed and used in order to identify, prioritise, plan and implement improvements and innovations.

RADAR percentage - quick score prediction for this Criterion:

Decision 1 Approach Score	Decision 2 Deployment Score	Decision 3 Refinement Score	Predicted Overall %
			_____ % (=Total of Decision 1+2+3)

Step 1 Understanding the EFQM Model

Excellent organisations design, manage and improve processes, products and services to generate increasing value for customers and other stakeholders.

They assess their performance and manage the five critical areas shown in the Criterion-parts on the right.

Customer Focus

5a Designed & managed to **Optimise Business Stakeholder Value**

5c Promote and Market

5e Enhance relationships

Criterion 6 Customer Results

5b Designed & managed to **Create Optimum Value for Customers**

5d Produce, Deliver and Service

Take to Market

Design and Manage

Step 2 Summarise your management methods and their impact on Processes, Products and Services criteria

2.1 Map your Enablers List/map the processes and approaches (groups of processes) that you have that impact on these Criterion parts	2.2 Summarise Deployment Log to what extent do you intend to deploy each approach and how you can demonstrate you've done it?	2.3 List Reviews and Refinements Log how often you review these approaches and the overall mix of approaches? What refinements have been made?

2.1 Map your Enablers	2.2 Summarise Deployment	2.3 List Reviews and Refinements
List/map the processes and approaches (groups of processes) that you have that impact on these Criterion parts	Log to what extent do you intend to deploy each approach and how you can demonstrate you've done it?	Log how often you review these approaches and the overall mix of approaches? What refinements have been made?

Step 3 Review the good practices of others

Our experience with Award winners leads us to conclude that the following are generically good practices. You may find these useful to review, along with your own organisational specific research and learning on good practice approaches, before you conclude your analysis of Strengths and Areas for Improvement for this Criterion.

In our analyses we find that high performing organisations put emphasis on:

1   Having high-level process maps to describe the structure, linkages and operation of all key processes.
2   Having assigned owners, responsibilities and standards for all processes.
3   Developing products and services in a structured way.
4   Having innovation management systems.
5   Using valid process level performance targeting techniques.
6   Understanding and communicating the value proposition, features and benefits of the organisation's products and services to current and potential marketplaces.
7   Monitoring and overseeing that promises made are delivered.
8   Ensuring ever improving product and service consistency.
9   Managing products and services throughout their entire life-cycle considering environmental impacts where appropriate.
10 Developing customer relationships and an acuity for diagnosing unmet customer or market needs, as well as general process improvements.

From my own experiences I would also include an emphasis on:
List your own research in your sector/organisation

Step 4 Conclude an analysis of your key Strengths and Areas for Improvement for this Criterion

Strengths	Areas for Improvement

Decision 1: Quick score the Approaches used in this Criterion				
We don't manage this very formally.	We know what we need to do; some structured approaches are now in place.	Relevant, *soundly based* approaches in place, in many areas.	Proven, sound, refined, well *integrated* approaches in most areas.	Approaches can be shown to be at world-class role model levels.

0	1	2	3	4	5	6	7	8	9	10	11	12	13	14	15	16	17	18	19	20	21	22	23	24	25	26	27	28	29	30	31	32	33

Keep in mind your summary of +/-'s and tick a single number above, remember that:

- *Soundly based:* means the approaches have clear rationales, defined processes and focus on stakeholder needs.
- *Integrated:* means that the approaches support policy and strategy and are linked to other approaches where appropriate.

Decision 2: Quick score Deployment of the approaches used in this Criterion				
We've not deployed our ideas in a structured way.	The approaches are *implemented* to less than 25% of their intended potential.	We can show evidence of *implementation* to 50% of the full potential.	Clear and *Systematic implementation* to 75% of full potential across all areas.	Our approaches are robustly *implemented* to full potential in all relevant areas.

0	1	2	3	4	5	6	7	8	9	10	11	12	13	14	15	16	17	18	19	20	21	22	23	24	25	26	27	28	29	30	31	32	33

Keep in mind your summary of +/-'s and tick a single number above, remember that:

- *Implemented:* means the extent to which the approach is put into effective use/deployment.
- *Systematic:* means that as well as being deployed, you judge that the deployment was carried out in a structured way with the method used to ensure deployment being itself planned and executed soundly.

Decision 3: Quick score the Assessment and Refinement of this Criterion

We do not do assess and refine in a structured way.	Occasional measurement and review of the approaches used in the Criterion.	Good evidence of measurement, review, learning from others and improvement.	Regular, effective measurement and process level learning is undertaken. Creativity, innovation & improvement is evident.	All approaches are regularly refined, learning and innovation can be comprehensively demonstrated.

0	1	2	3	4	5	6	7	8	9	10	11	12	13	14	15	16	17	18	19	20	21	22	23	24	25	26	27	28	29	30	31	32	33

Keep in mind your summary of +/-'s and tick a single number above, remember that:

- *Measurement:* means the extent to which regular and appropriate measurement of the effectiveness and efficiency of the approach and its deployment takes place.
- *Learning:* has a scope that includes the extent to which knowledge transfer takes place to identify good practice focussed improvement opportunities and how creativity is used to stimulate ideas.
- *Improvement:* means the extent to which the output from measurement and learning is analysed and used in order to identify, prioritise, plan and implement improvements and innovations.

RADAR percentage - quick score prediction for this Criterion:

Decision 1 Approach Score	Decision 2 Deployment Score	Decision 3 Refinement Score	Predicted Overall %
			_____ % (=Total of Decision 1+2+3)

Step 1 Understanding the EFQM Model

Excellent organisations measure, achieve and manage based on a portfolio of perception results and related indicators, they:

- Develop and agree a set of performance indicators and related outcomes to determine the successful deployment of their strategy and supporting policies, based on the needs and expectations of their customers.
- Set clear targets for Key Results based on the needs and expectations of their customers, in line with their chosen strategy.
- Demonstrate positive or sustained good customer results over at least three years.
- Clearly understand the underlying reasons and drivers of observed trends and the impact these results will have on other performance indicators and related outcomes.
- Anticipate future performance and results.
- Understand how the Key Results they achieve compared to similar organisations and use this data where relevant for target setting.
- Segment results to understand the experience, needs and expectations of specific customer groups.

6b Performance Indicators → **6a Perception Measures**

Internal, predictive measures   Customer views

←

Performance Drivers   **Feedback From the Stakeholder**

Step 2 Create a data review summary for the Customer Results criteria

2.1 List the **Data/Measures** you have and use (Note any that may not be accurate, timely or comprehensive)	2.2 Analyse **3 yr. Trends** (+/0/-)	2.3 **Target Achievement** (+/0/-	2.4 Comparison to **WC/BIC*** (+/0/-)	2.5 Related **Key Enablers**

2.1 List the **Data/Measures** you have and use (Note any that may not be accurate, timely or comprehensive)	2.2 Analyse **3 yr. Trends** (+/0/-)	2.3 **Target Achievement** (+/0/-)	2.4 Comparison to **WC/BIC*** (+/0/-)	2.5 Related **Key Enablers**

2.6 List any results that you believe are important but for which you have no data/records:

(*World Class competitor or Best in Class comparison to be demonstrable with real data)

Step 3 Review the good practices of others

Our experience with Award winners leads us to conclude that the following are generically good practices. You may find these useful to review, along with your own organisational specific research and learning on good practice approaches, before you conclude your analysis of Strengths and Areas for Improvement for this Criterion.

In our analyses we find that high performing organisations put emphasis on:

1   Seeing themselves as their Customers and Potential Customers see them.
2   Understand both the needs and expectations of those who they regard as Customers.
3   Have a focus on the key data sets that are the most important to manage.
4   Constantly hunt for latent or unmet Customer needs.
5   Understand what is likely to drive/enable future Customer loyalty and satisfaction.
6   Identify and manage Enablers and related data to help drive performance in areas of the business likely to drive enhanced Customer Results.
7   Have clarity on the reasons for choosing the benchmark organisations/comparative data sets that are used.
8   Track and act on both long and short-term priorities for customers.

From my own experiences I would also include an emphasis on:

List your own research in your sector/organisation

Step 4 Conclude an analysis of your key Strengths and Areas for Improvement for this Criterion

Strengths	Areas for Improvement

RADAR Estimate for Customer Results Criterion

Decision 1: Quick score the Relevance and Usability of the data you have				
We don't have *relevant* data.	*Few-Some relevant* measurements.	*Some-Many* measurements of relevant parameters, data is well segmented and integrity is proven in most areas.	Regular, credible measurements in *Most* areas that can be shown to be of proven *relevance* for the stakeholders being tracked.	Regular measurement of *All relevant* parameters and stakeholders, data is timely, reliable and accurate

0	1	2	3	4	5	6	7	8	9	10	11	12	13	14	15	16	17	18	19	20	21	22	23	24	25	26	27	28	29	30	31	32	33

Keep in mind your summary of +/-'s and tick a single number above, remember that:

- *Relevant* means proven to be of value to the appropriate stakeholder(s) of, and strategically comprehensive for, the Criterion being assessed.

Decision 2: Quick score the trend and target performance of your Achievements for this Criterion				
On balance, negative trends exist.	*Some* positive trends and achievement of our targets. The outcomes were not just "good luck"	Positive trends over 3+ years and achievement of our own targets, in *many (50%+)* areas. Targets achieved for key results.	Positive trends over 3+ years and achievement of our own targets in at least *3/4 of the results*. Most results caused by own efforts	Strongly positive trends in *all relevant results* for 3+ years. Excellent comparisons against own targets. *Causal* links clear

0	1	2	3	4	5	6	7	8	9	10	11	12	13	14	15	16	17	18	19	20	21	22	23	24	25	26	27	28	29	30	31	32	33

Keep in mind your summary of +/-'s and tick a single number above, remember that:

- *Cause*, means that the link between the outcome achieved and what enabled it is understood and manageable.
- *Trends* should be demonstrable by readily available data sources.

Decision 3: Quick score How well your performance compares/ "benchmarks" with others for **this Criterion**				
We do not know.	Few external comparisons made or favourable. Some internal comparisons beginning.	Favourable external performance comparisons on at least half the *key results.*	Favourable comparisons with external organisations in *most key* relevant areas	Excellent comparisons with world class competitors and/ or best in class organisations.

0	1	2	3	4	5	6	7	8	9	10	11	12	13	14	15	16	17	18	19	20	21	22	23	24	25	26	27	28	29	30	31	32	33

Keep in mind your summary of +/-'s and tick a single number above, remember that:

- *Key results* refer to those that you strategically identify and prioritise as the most important.

RADAR percentage - quick score prediction for this Criterion:

Decision 1 Relevance Score	**Decision 2** Achievement Score	**Decision 3** Comparison Score	**Predicted Overall %**
			_____ % (=Total of Decision 1+2+3)

Step 1 Understanding the EFQM Model

Excellent organisations measure, achieve and manage based on a portfolio of perception results and related indicators, they:

- Develop and agree a set of performance indicators and related outcomes to determine the successful deployment of their strategy and supporting policies, based on the needs and expectations of their people.
- Set clear targets for Key Results based on the needs and expectations of their people, in line with their chosen strategy.
- Demonstrate positive or sustained good people and results over at least three years.
- Clearly understand the underlying reasons and drivers of observed trends and the impact these results will have on other performance indicators and related outcomes.
- Anticipate future performance and results.
- Understand how the Key Results they achieve compared to similar organisations and use this data where relevant for target setting.
- Segment results to understand the experience, needs and expectations of specific people groups within their organisation.

7b Performance Indicators	→	**7a Perception Measures**
Predictor measures		Employee views
	←	
Performance Drivers		**Feedback From the Stakeholder**

Step 2 Create a data review summary for the People Results criteria

2.1 List the **Data/Measures** you have and use (Note any that may not be accurate, timely or comprehensive)	2.2 Analyse **3 yr. Trends** (+/0/-)	2.3 **Target Achievement** (+/0/-	2.4 Comparison to **WC/BIC*** (+/0/-)	2.5 Related **Key Enablers**

2.1 List the **Data/Measures** you have and use (Note any that may not be accurate, timely or comprehensive)	2.2 Analyse **3 yr. Trends** (+/0/-)	2.3 **Target Achievement** (+/0/-)	2.4 Comparison to **WC/BIC*** (+/0/-)	2.5 Related **Key Enablers**

2.6 List any results that you believe are important but for which you have no data/records:

(*World Class competitor or Best in Class comparison to be demonstrable with real data)

Step 3 Review the good practices of others

Our experience with Award winners leads us to conclude that the following are generically good practices. You may find these useful to review, along with your own organisational specific research and learning on good practice approaches before you conclude your analysis of Strengths and Areas for Improvement for this Criterion.

In our analyses we find that high performing organisations put emphasis on:

1   Seeing themselves as their People see them.
2   Segmenting the analysis of people data by organisational units/levels/sectors, to ensure that insights, resources, and improvement activity are appropriately targeted.
3   Being seen to understand/act upon the reasons for successes and shortfalls.
4   Understanding what is likely to drive/enable motivation and satisfaction needed for the future and there-by have a focus on the Enablers to review and manage.
5   Understanding what will be needed to gain or retain "talent" in the future, if it is different to that of today, and how this may effect the tracking and monitoring of People satisfaction and motivation.
6   Have clarity on the reasons for choosing the benchmark organisations/comparative data sets that are used.
7   Track and act on both long and short-term priorities for People.

From my own experiences I would also include an emphasis on:
List your own research in your sector/organisation

Step 4 Conclude an analysis of your key Strengths and Areas for Improvement for this Criterion

Strengths	Areas for Improvement

Decision 1: Quick score the Relevance and Usability of the data you have

We don't have *relevant* data.	*Few-Some relevant* measurements.	*Some-Many* measurements of relevant parameters, data is well segmented and integrity is proven in most areas.	Regular, credible measurements in *Most* areas that can be shown to be of proven *relevance* for the stakeholders being tracked.	Regular measurement of *All relevant* parameters and stakeholders, data is timely, reliable and accurate

0	1	2	3	4	5	6	7	8	9	10	11	12	13	14	15	16	17	18	19	20	21	22	23	24	25	26	27	28	29	30	31	32	33

Keep in mind your summary of +/-'s and tick a single number above, remember that:

- *Relevant* means proven to be of value to the appropriate stakeholder(s) of, and strategically comprehensive for, the Criterion being assessed.

Decision 2: Quick score the trend and target performance of your Achievements for this Criterion

On balance, negative trends exist.	*Some* positive trends and achievement of our targets. The outcomes were not just "good luck"	Positive trends over 3+ years and achievement of our own targets, in *many (50%+)* areas. Targets achieved for key results.	Positive trends over 3+ years and achievement of our own targets in at least *3/4 of the results*. Most results caused by own efforts	Strongly positive trends in *all relevant results* for 3+ years. Excellent comparisons against own targets *Causal* links clear

0	1	2	3	4	5	6	7	8	9	10	11	12	13	14	15	16	17	18	19	20	21	22	23	24	25	26	27	28	29	30	31	32	33

Keep in mind your summary of +/-'s and tick a single number above, remember that:

- *Cause*, means that the link between the outcome achieved and what enabled it is understood and manageable.
- *Trends* should be demonstrable by readily available data sources.

Decision 3: Quick score How well your performance compares/"benchmarks" with others for **this Criterion**				
We do not know.	Few external comparisons made or favourable. Some internal comparisons beginning.	Favourable external performance comparisons on at least half the *key results.*	Favourable comparisons with external organisations in *most key* relevant areas	Excellent comparisons with world class competitors and/ or best in class organisations.

0	1	2	3	4	5	6	7	8	9	10	11	12	13	14	15	16	17	18	19	20	21	22	23	24	25	26	27	28	29	30	31	32	33

Keep in mind your summary of +/-'s and tick a single number above, remember that:

- *Key results* refer to those that you strategically identify and prioritise as the most important.

RADAR percentage - quick score prediction for this Criterion:

Decision 1 Relevance Score	**Decision 2** Achievement Score	**Decision 3** Comparison Score	**Predicted Overall** %
			_____% (=Total of Decision 1+2+3)

Step 1 Understanding the EFQM Model

Excellent organisations measure, achieve and manage based on a portfolio of perception results and related indicators, they:

- Develop and agree a set of performance indicators and related outcomes to determine the successful deployment of their societal and ecological strategy and related policies, based on the needs and expectations of relevant external societal stakeholders.
- Set clear targets for Key Results based on the needs and expectations of their external societal stakeholders, in line with their chosen strategy.
- Demonstrate positive or sustained good societal results over at least three years.
- Clearly understand the underlying reasons and drivers of observed trends and the impact these results will have on other performance indicators and related outcomes.
- Anticipate future performance and results.
- Understand how the Key Results they achieve compared to similar organisations and use this data where relevant for target setting.
- Segment results to understand the experience, needs and expectations of specific stakeholders within society.

8b Performance Indicators	→	8a Perception Measures
Internal predictive, measures		Society's views
Performance Drivers	←	**Feedback**

Step 2 Create a data review summary for the Society Results criteria

2.1 List the **Data/Measures** you have and use (Note any that may not be accurate, timely or comprehensive)	2.2 Analyse **3 yr. Trends** (+/0/-)	2.3 **Target Achievement** (+/0/-	2.4 Comparison to **WC/BIC*** (+/0/-)	2.5 Related **Key Enablers**

2.1 List the **Data/Measures** you have and use (Note any that may not be accurate, timely or comprehensive)	2.2 Analyse **3 yr. Trends** (+/0/-)	2.3 **Target Achievement** (+/0/-)	2.4 Comparison to **WC/BIC*** (+/0/-)	2.5 Related **Key Enablers**

2.6 List any results that you believe are important but for which you have no data/records:

*World Class competitor or Best in Class comparison to be demonstrable with real data)

Step 3 Review the good practices of others

Our experience with Award winners leads us to conclude that the following are generically good practices. You may find these useful to review, along with your own organisational specific research and learning on good practice approaches, before you conclude your analysis of Strengths and Areas for Improvement for this Criterion.

In our analyses we find that high performing organisations put emphasis on:

1   Understanding the risk/opportunities that Societal performance may create for the organisations "Brand".
2   Understanding and obtaining broad stakeholder engagement.
3   Having governance processes that embrace and measure Human Rights, Labour Practices, The Environment, Fair Operating Practices, Product Responsibility, Consumer Issues, and Community Involvement and Development.
4   Identifying a range of societal perception measures and tracking data which will provide insights as to how their organisation functions and is perceived in the societies it operates in, or impacts upon.
5   Understand the causes of trends, over time, in the results.
6   Compare their organisation's societal performance to targets and understand/act upon the reasons for successes and shortfalls.
7   Compare their performance to that of others/'best in class' organisations.
8   Segment the analysis of societal data by local, regional, national or global dimensions, as appropriate to the operations/products/services involved.

From my own experiences I would also include an emphasis on:

List your own research in your sector/organisation

Step 4 Conclude an analysis of your key Strengths and Areas for Improvement for this Criterion

Strengths	Areas for Improvement

RADAR Estimate for Society Results Criterion

Decision 1: Quick score the Relevance and Usability of the data you have

We don't have *relevant* data.	*Few-Some relevant* measurements.	*Some-Many* measurements of relevant parameters, data is well segmented and integrity is proven in most areas.	Regular, credible measurements in *Most* areas that can be shown to be of proven *relevance* for the stakeholders being tracked.	Regular measurement of *All relevant* parameters and stakeholders, data is timely, reliable and accurate

0	1	2	3	4	5	6	7	8	9	10	11	12	13	14	15	16	17	18	19	20	21	22	23	24	25	26	27	28	29	30	31	32	33

Keep in mind your summary of +/-'s and tick a single number above, remember that:

- *Relevant* means proven to be of value to the appropriate stakeholder(s) of, and strategically comprehensive for, the Criterion being assessed.

Decision 2: Quick score the trend and target performance of your Achievements for this Criterion

On balance, negative trends exist.	*Some* positive trends and achievement of our targets. The outcomes were not just "good luck"	Positive trends over 3+ years and achievement of our own targets, in *many (50%+)* areas. Targets achieved for key results.	Positive trends over 3+ years and achievement of our own targets in at least *3/4 of the results*. Most results caused by own efforts	Strongly positive trends in *all relevant results* for 3+ years. Excellent comparisons against own targets. *Causal* links clear

0	1	2	3	4	5	6	7	8	9	10	11	12	13	14	15	16	17	18	19	20	21	22	23	24	25	26	27	28	29	30	31	32	33

Keep in mind your summary of +/-'s and tick a single number above, remember that:

- *Cause*, means that the link between the outcome achieved and what enabled it is understood and manageable.
- *Trends* should be demonstrable by readily available data sources.

Decision 3: Quick score	How well your performance compares/"benchmarks" with others for **this Criterion**			
We do not know.	Few external comparisons made or favourable. Some internal comparisons beginning.	Favourable external performance comparisons on at least half the *key results.*	Favourable comparisons with external organisations in *most key* relevant areas	Excellent comparisons with world class competitors and/ or best in class organisations.

0	1	2	3	4	5	6	7	8	9	10	11	12	13	14	15	16	17	18	19	20	21	22	23	24	25	26	27	28	29	30	31	32	33

Keep in mind your summary of +/-'s and tick a single number above, remember that:

- *Key results* refer to those that you strategically identify and prioritise as the most important.

RADAR percentage - quick score prediction for this Criterion:

Decision 1 Relevance Score	**Decision 2** Achievement Score	**Decision 3** Comparison Score	**Predicted Overall** **%**
			_____ % (=Total of Decision 1+2+3)

Step 1 Understanding the EFQM Model

Excellent organisations measure, achieve and manage based on a portfolio of perception results and related indicators, they:

- Develop and agree a set of key financial and non-financial results to determine the successful deployment of their strategy and supporting policies, based on the needs and expectations of their key stakeholders.
- Set clear targets for Key Results based on the needs and expectations of their key stakeholders, in line with their chosen strategy
- Demonstrate positive or sustained good key results over at least three years.
- Clearly understand the underlying reasons and drivers of observed trends and the impact these results will have on other performance indicators and related outcomes.
- Anticipate future performance and results.
- Understand how the Key Results they achieve compared to similar organisations and use this data where relevant for target setting.
- Segment results to understand the performance levels and strategic outcomes achieved within specific areas of the organisation.

9b Key Performance Indicators

Operational Performance

9a Key Strategic Outcomes

Financial and non Financial

Performance Enabler Oversight

Feedback on Strategy Deployment

Step 2 Create a data review summary for the Key Results criteria

2.1 List the **Data/Measures** you have and use (Note any that may not be accurate, timely or comprehensive)	2.2 Analyse **3 yr. Trends** (+/0/-)	2.3 **Target Achievement** (+/0/-	2.4 Comparison to **WC/BIC*** (+/0/-)	2.5 Related **Key Enablers**

2.1 List the **Data/Measures** you have and use (Note any that may not be accurate, timely or comprehensive)	2.2 Analyse **3 yr. Trends** (+/0/-)	2.3 **Target Achievement** (+/0/-	2.4 Comparison to **WC/BIC*** (+/0/-)	2.5 Related **Key Enablers**

2.6 List any results that you believe are important but for which you have no data/records:

(*World Class competitor or Best in Class comparison to be demonstrable with real data)

Step 3 Review the good practices of others

Our experience with Award winners leads us to conclude that the following are generically good practices. You may find these useful to review, along with your own organisational specific research and learning on good practice approaches, before you conclude your analysis of Strengths and Areas for Improvement for this Criterion.

In our analyses we find that high performing organisations put emphasis on:

1 Defining and agreeing with key stakeholders the relevant financial measures that will track the deployment/achievement of their chosen strategies. (these will typically include profit and loss, balance sheet, cash flow, and shareholder value-added in commercial organisations, and performance against budgets in non-commercial areas).

2 Defining a set of key non-financial measures that are indicative of success with the key strategic aims defined in the organisation's Strategy and Policies (depending on the type of organisation and its strategy these may include measures such as market share, innovation rates, learning, breakthrough project activities, flexibility, and responsiveness to change).

3 Track and understand the causes of trends, over time, in the results above.

4 Compare their performance to their strategies, targets and plans, in order to understand/act upon the reasons for successes and shortfalls.

5 Understand what is likely to drive/enable future success.

6 Segment their data by organisational units/level/sectors to ensure that insights, resources, and improvement activity are appropriately targeted.

7 Compare their performance to that of competitors and/or 'best in class' organisations.

From my own experiences I would also include an emphasis on:

List your own research in your sector/organisation

Step 4 Conclude an analysis of your key Strengths and Areas for Improvement for this Criterion

Strengths	Areas for Improvement

Decision 1: Quick score the Relevance and Usability of the data you have				
We don't have *relevant* data.	*Few-Some relevant* measurements.	*Some-Many* measurements of relevant parameters, data is well segmented and integrity is proven in most areas.	Regular, credible measurements in *Most* areas that can be shown to be of proven *relevance* for the stakeholders being tracked.	Regu ar measurement of *All relevant* parameters and stakeholders, data is timely, reliable and accurate

0	1	2	3	4	5	6	7	8	9	10	11	12	13	14	15	16	17	18	19	20	21	22	23	24	25	26	27	28	29	30	31	32	33

Keep in mind your summary of +/-'s and tick a single number above, remember that:

- *Relevant* means proven to be of value to the appropriate stakeholder(s) of, and strategically comprehensive for, the Criterion being assessed.

Decision 2: Quick score the trend and target performance of your Achievements for this Criterion				
On balance, negative trends exist.	*Some* positive trends and achievement of our targets. The outcomes were not just "good luck"	Positive trends over 3+ years and achievement of our own targets, in *many (50%+)* areas. Targets achieved for key results.	Positive trends over 3+ years and achievement of our own targets in at least *3/4 of the results*. Most results caused by own efforts	Strongly positive trends in *all relevant results* for 3+ years. Excellent comparisons against own targets. *Causal* links clear

0	1	2	3	4	5	6	7	8	9	10	11	12	13	14	15	16	17	18	19	20	21	22	23	24	25	26	27	28	29	3C	31	32	33

Keep in mind your summary of +/-'s and tick a single number above, remember that:

- *Cause*, means that the link between the outcome achieved and what enabled it is understood and manageable.
- *Trends* should be demonstrable by readily available data sources.

Decision 3: Quick score How well your performance compares/"benchmarks" with others for **this Criterion**				
We do not know.	Few external comparisons made or favourable. Some internal comparisons beginning.	Favourable external performance comparisons on at least half the *key results.*	Favourable comparisons with external organisations in *most key* relevant areas	Excellent comparisons with world class competitors and/ or best in class organisations.

0	1	2	3	4	5	6	7	8	9	10	11	12	13	14	15	16	17	18	19	20	21	22	23	24	25	26	27	28	29	30	31	32	33

Keep in mind your summary of +/-'s and tick a single number above, remember that:

- *Key results* refer to those that you strategically identify and prioritise as the most important.

RADAR percentage - quick score prediction for this Criterion:

Decision 1 Relevance Score	Decision 2 Achievement Score	Decision 3 Comparison Score	Predicted Overall %
			_____ % (=Total of Decision 1+2+3)

8. How do high performing organisations score against the EFQM Excellence Model?

What follows are a series of charts showing the scoring of the last publically released aggregate data (2007 to 2010) on the Applicants for the EFQM Excellence Award. The data is presented as the percentage of total Applicants ("y" axis) scoring in specific % bands for each Criterion ("x" axis).

What conclusions can be drawn from this data?

The following tables will help to show you where you sit in your journey towards Excellence in numerical terms.

You probably need to manage your own expectations carefully as analysis of these tables will have shown you that no applicant has ever scored more than 800 out of a possible 1000 points and only 8% have scored above 700. Many of the Applicant organisations score below 50% in several criteria; -even though, collectively, this data represents some of the highest scoring, robustly assessed Applicants in the world!

The percentage points you have scored in each of your quick score Criterion analyses in Section 7 w ll be comparable with the data in the Criterion graphs that follow. The overall point's analysis (the first chart titled "Total") shows the so-called "overall points" out of 1000 created in a full EFQM Assessment. This is a weighted analysis where scores in points are accrued as follows:

- The EFQM Model uses a scoring system based on 1000 points, 500 of which, or 50%, are allocated to the Enablers, and 500 of which are allocated to the four Results Criteria
- All five Enabler criteria are equally weighted at 100 points, e.g. A 40% score in the Leadership Criterion gives a contribution of 40 points out of a possible 1000 to the overall points score
- The same applies to the People and Society Results, e.g. 60% in Criterion 7, equates to a 60/1000 contribution.
- Criterion 6, Customer Results, and Criterion 9, Key Results are weighted at x1.5 so a 50% score in Criterion 6 gives a 75/1000 contribution.

What conclusions can be drawn from this data?

Analysis of some of the most successful organisations (those scoring in the 600-800 point bands) shows that some generic features/practices exist. So, as a final thought, here are some of the things that typically exist in a 600+ organisation:

- Leaders know what they expect and how they will realise it
- The value chain is optimised, stakeholders are 'engaged', feedback and follow up is systematic and responsive
- Future value chains are foreseen, Innovation is evident
- Speed is evident in the organisation. Cycle time is a key driver, rapid deployment can occur
- Stakeholder requirements and expectations are understood, targeted and balanced in both Enablers and Results
- The organisation and its stakeholders as a whole can answer these questions:
    - What are we passionate about?
    - What is our key economic driver?
    - What can/should we become best in the world at?
- There is an integration and synergy among all parts and processes of the organisation
- There is substantial evidence of a philosophy and on-going success with 'Assessment and Refinement' including:
    - Many cycles of improvement driven by measurement and learning
    - Learning from both inside and outside the organisation, and sharing of achievements and good practice
- and of course The results show favourable comparisons with "top" organisations, not averages, they have strongly positive trends and demonstratable achievement of targeted performance.

Total Point/1000 scores

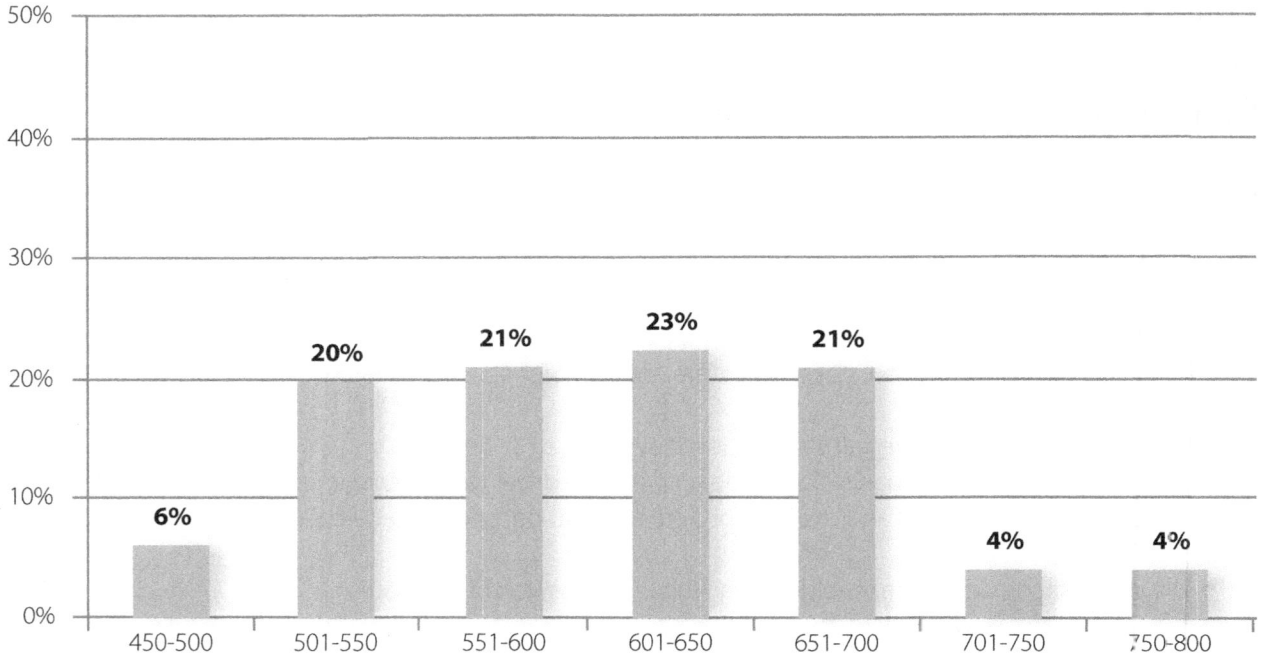

6%	20%	21%	23%	21%	4%	4%
450-500	501-550	551-600	601-650	651-700	701-750	750-800

1. Leadership

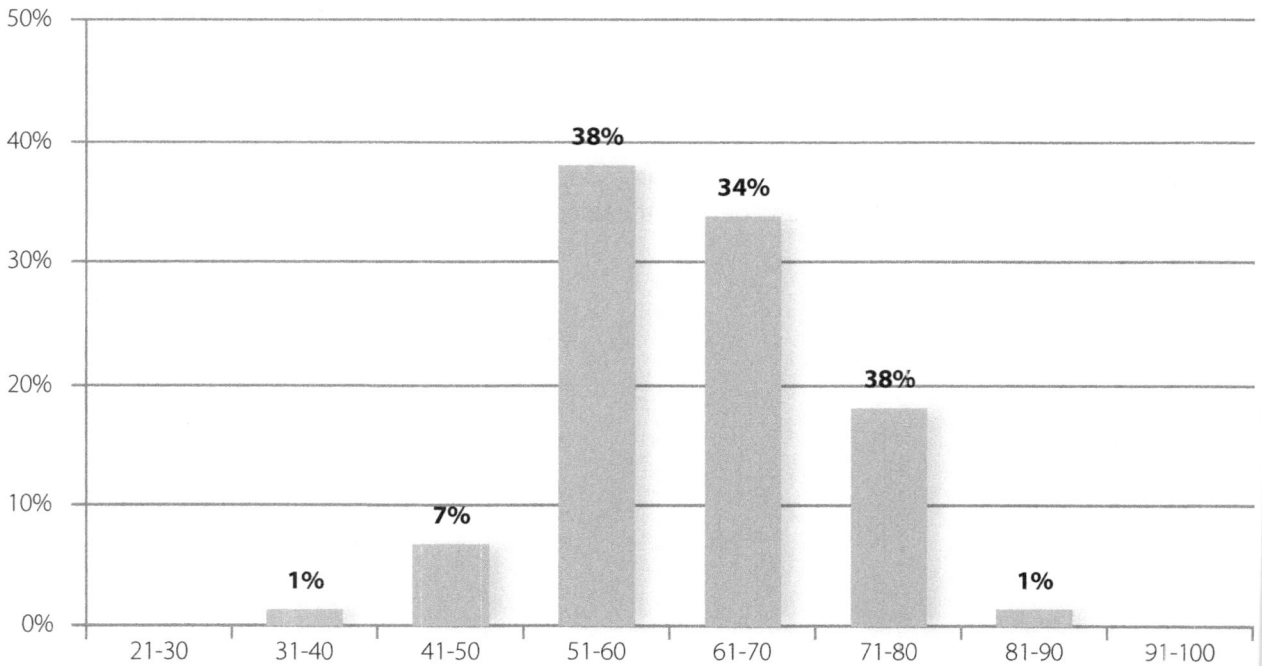

	1%	7%	38%	34%	38%	1%	
21-30	31-40	41-50	51-60	61-70	71-80	81-90	91-100

2. Strategy

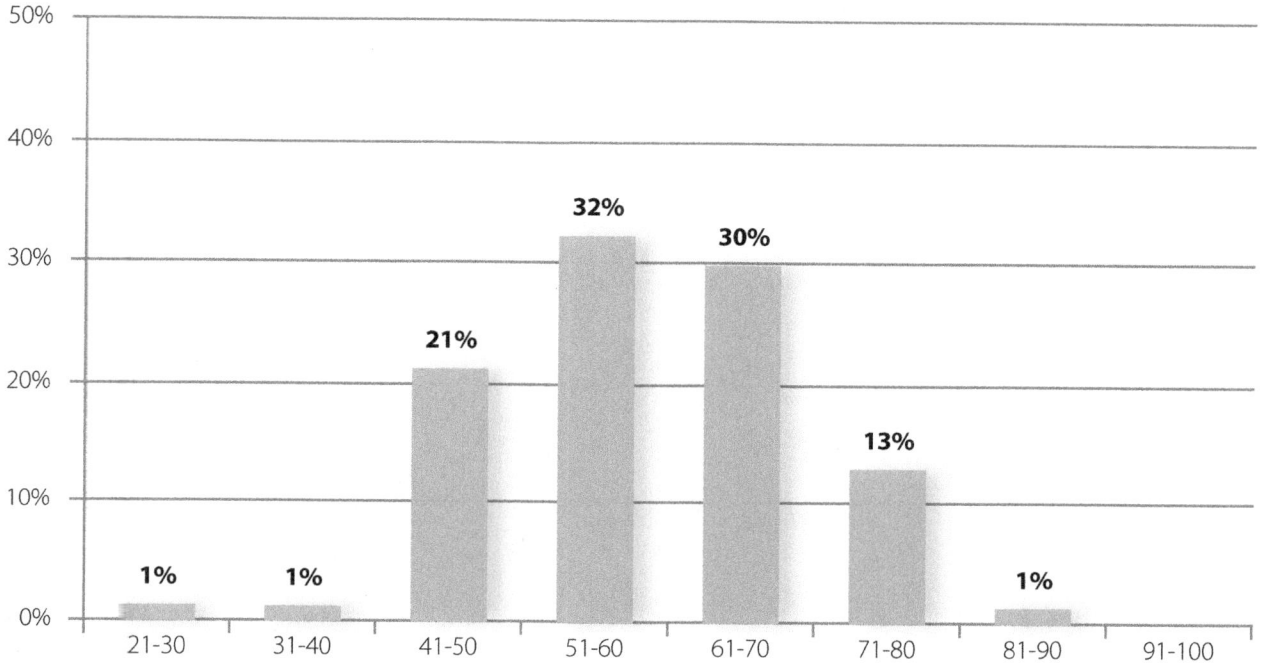

	21-30	31-40	41-50	51-60	61-70	71-80	81-90	91-100
	1%	1%	21%	32%	30%	13%	1%	

3. People

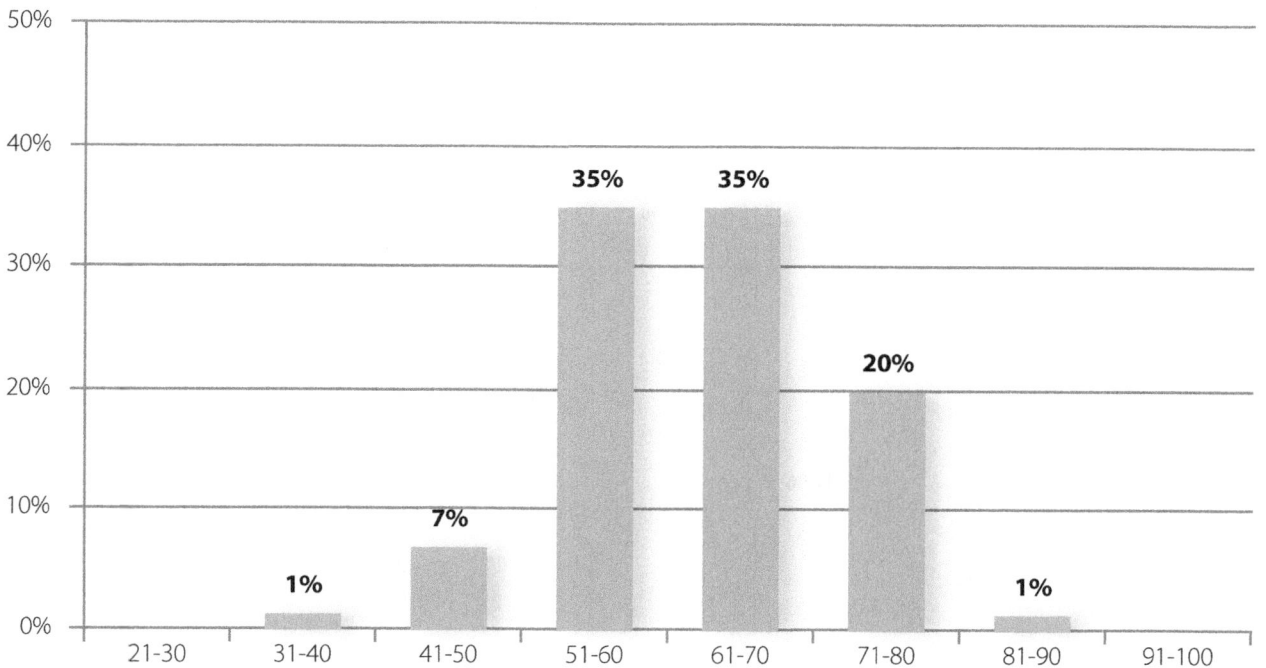

	21-30	31-40	41-50	51-60	61-70	71-80	81-90	91-100
		1%	7%	35%	35%	20%	1%	

4. Partnerships & Resources

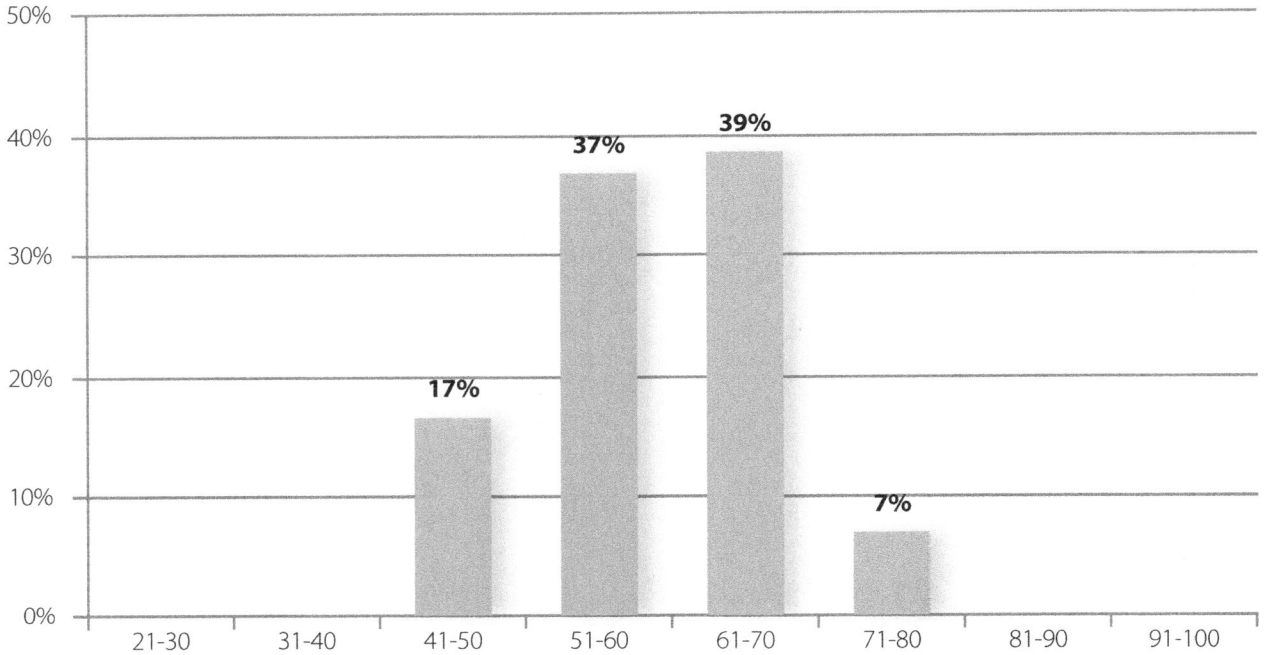

Range	Percentage
41-50	17%
51-60	37%
61-70	39%
71-80	7%

5. Processes, Products & Services

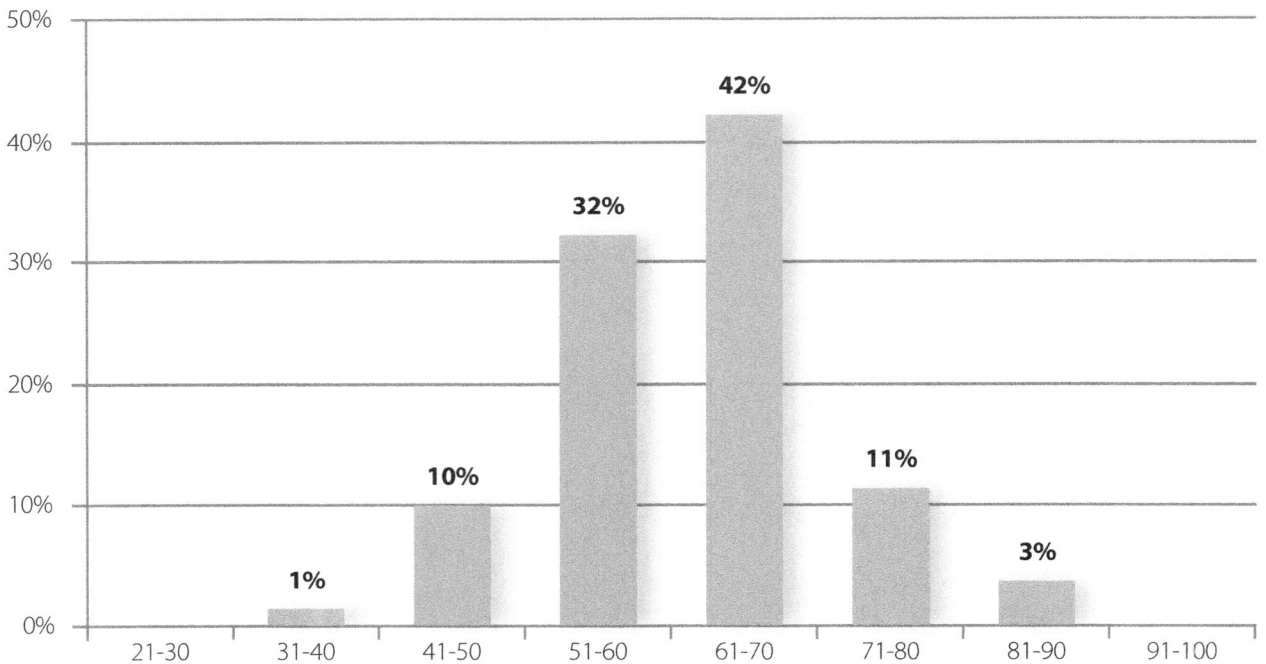

Range	Percentage
31-40	1%
41-50	10%
51-60	32%
61-70	42%
71-80	11%
81-90	3%

6. Customer Results

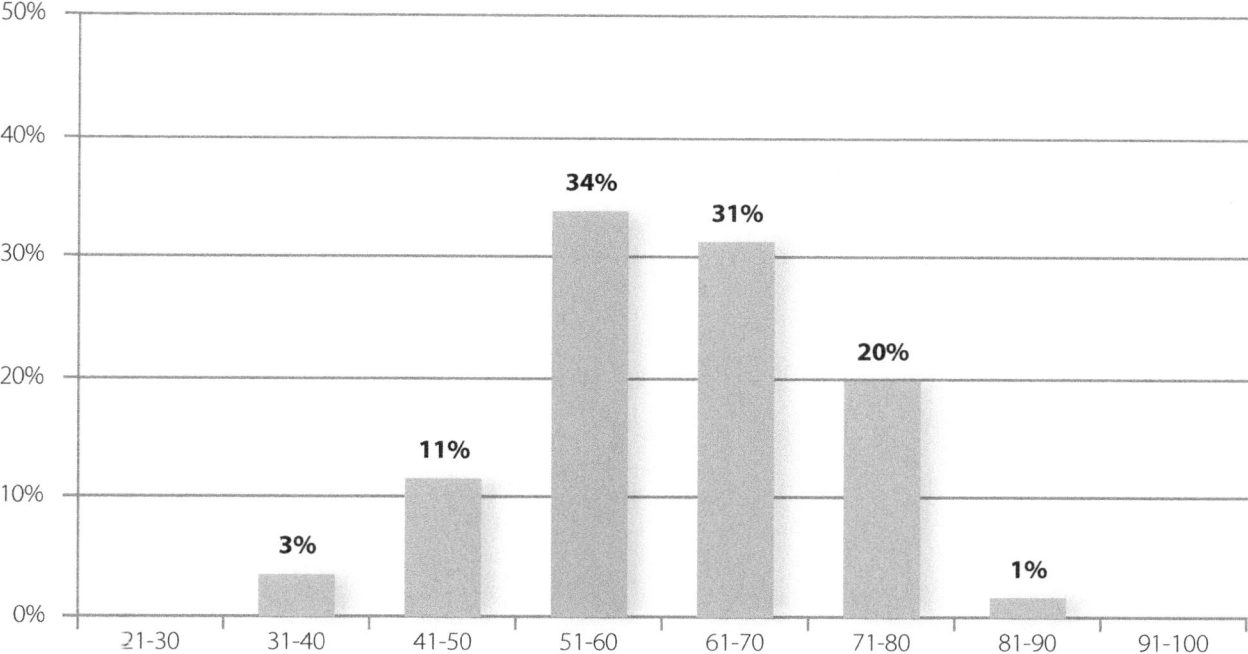

Range	Percentage
21-30	
31-40	3%
41-50	11%
51-60	34%
61-70	31%
71-80	20%
81-90	1%
91-100	

7. People Results

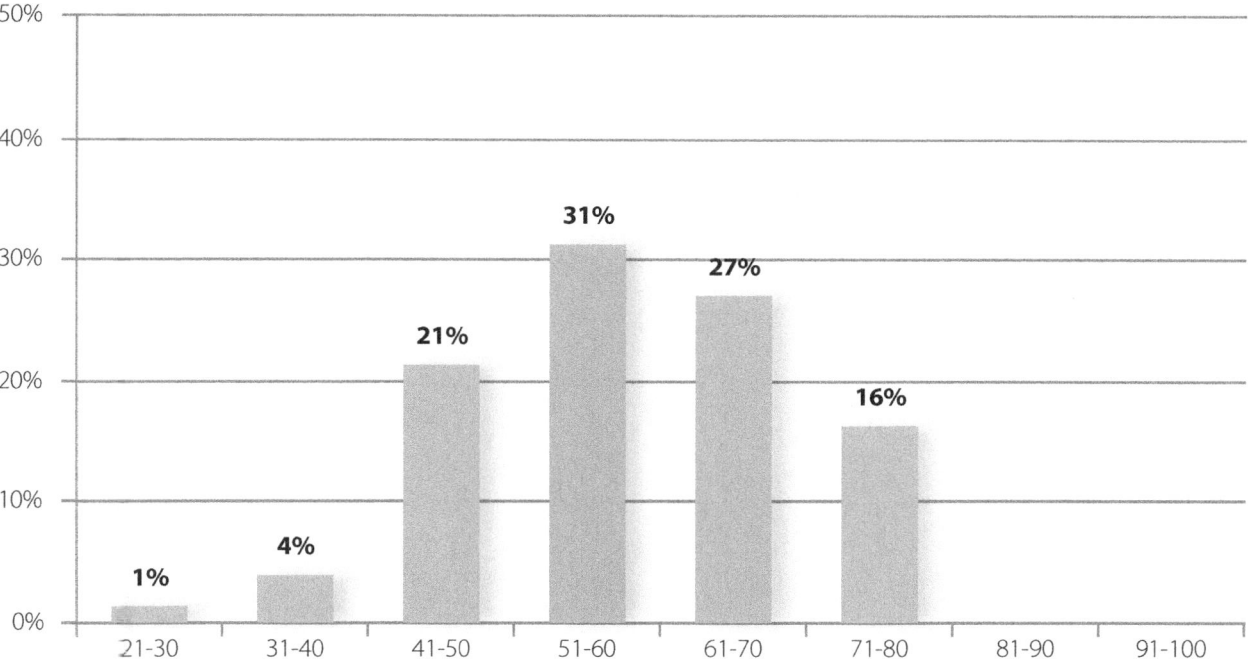

Range	Percentage
21-30	1%
31-40	4%
41-50	21%
51-60	31%
61-70	27%
71-80	16%
81-90	
91-100	

8. Society Results

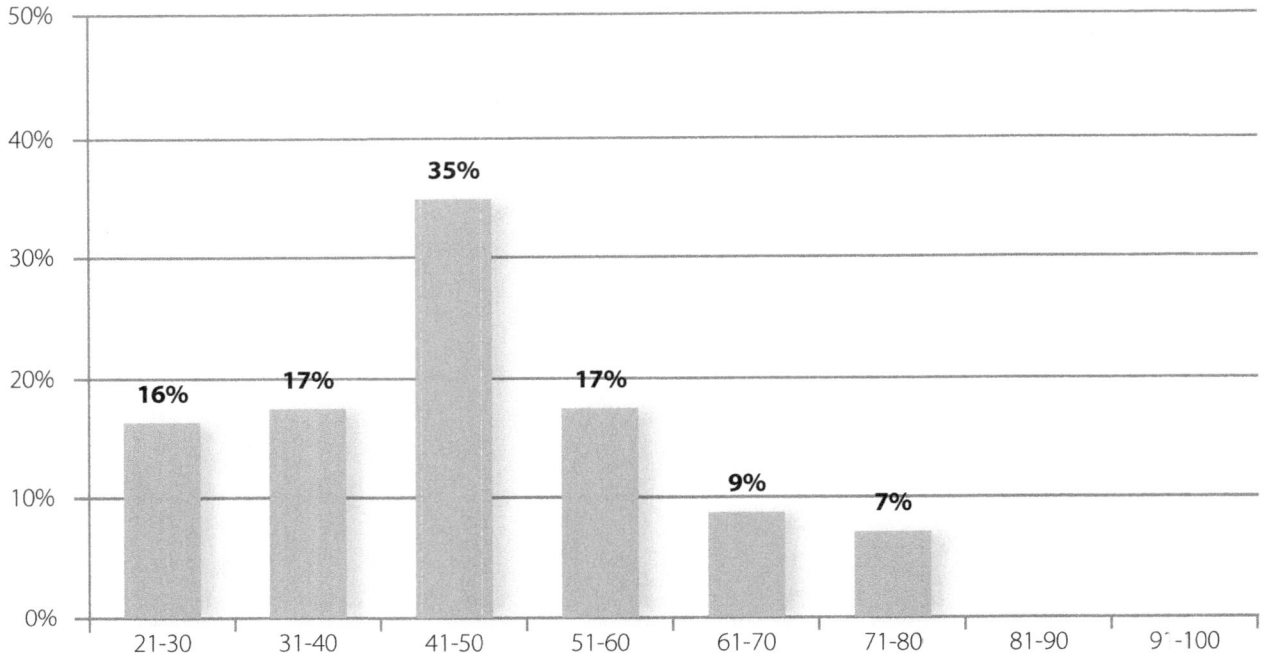

Range	Percentage
21-30	16%
31-40	17%
41-50	35%
51-60	17%
61-70	9%
71-80	7%
81-90	
91-100	

9. Key Results

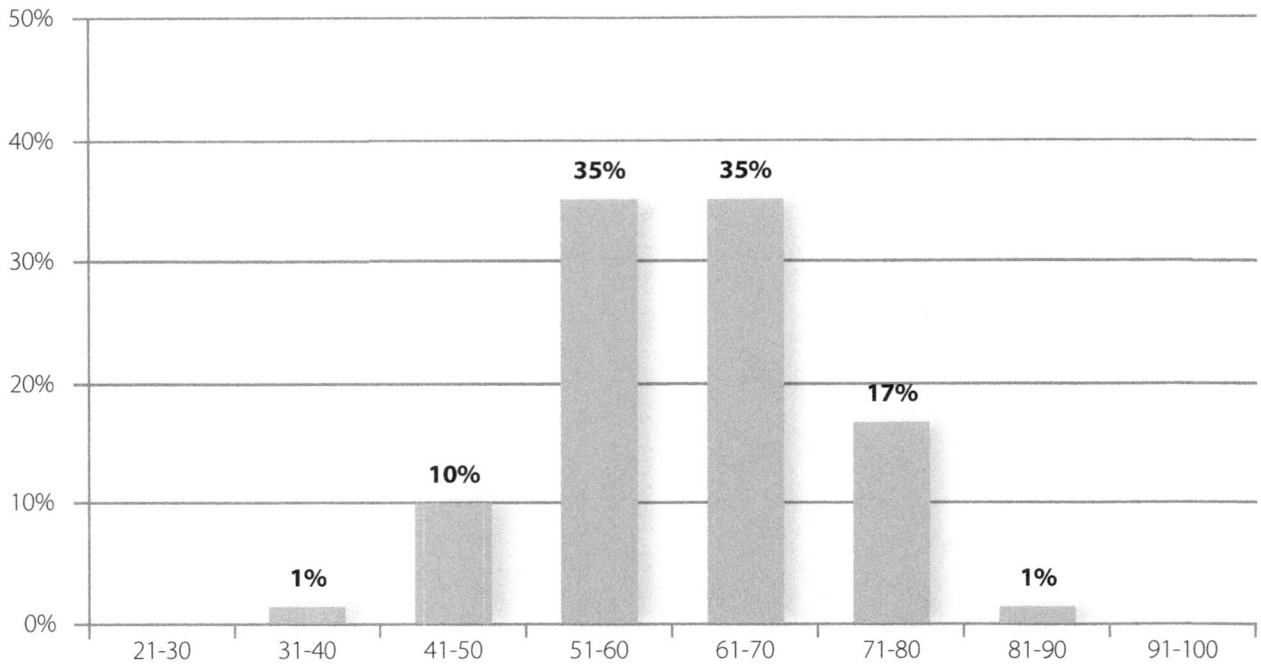

Range	Percentage
21-30	
31-40	1%
41-50	10%
51-60	35%
61-70	35%
71-80	17%
81-90	1%
91-100	

Highest/Average Per Criterion

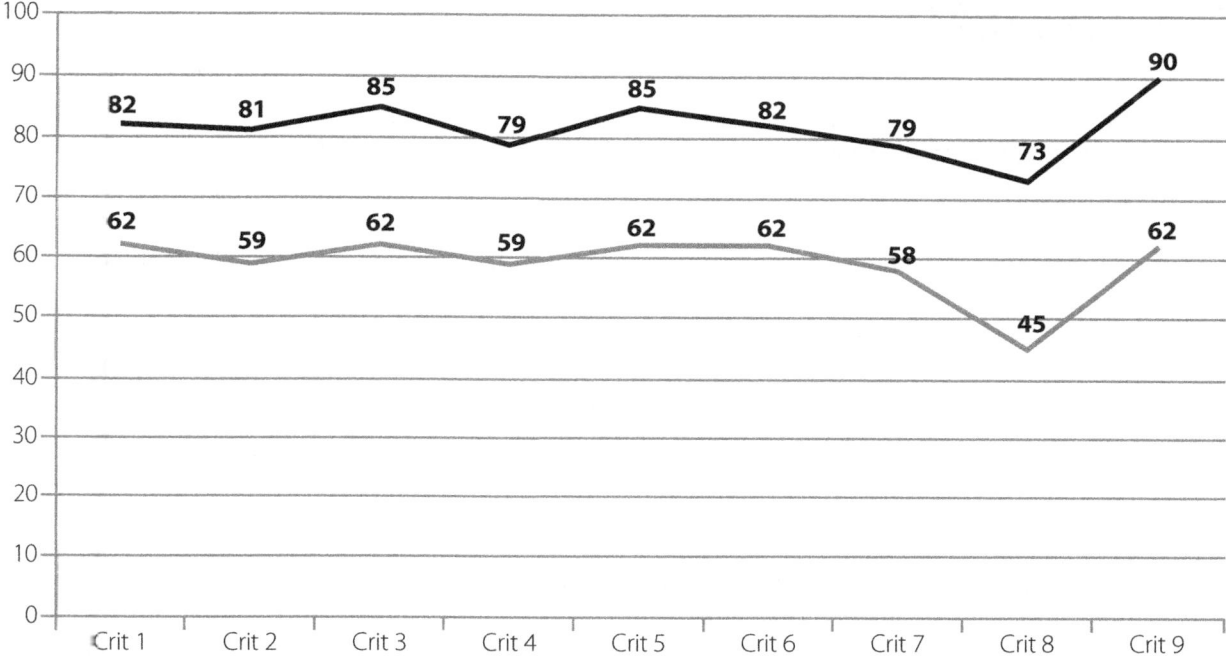

Legend:
- **Highest**
- Average

Appendix 1
What is EFQM?

Key Facts

EFQM is a Not for Profit membership foundation for organisations, small and large, public and private, around the globe. For over twenty years they have "shared what works" between their member organisations as a way help them implement their strategies. The EFQM Excellence Model provides the common framework and language that facilitates the effective sharing of information; transcending sectorial, cultural and maturity barriers.

EFQM operates the EFQM Excellence Award and other related recognition schemes. The EFQM member network is over 500 organisations in 55 countries and 50 industries, it is co-ordinated by a small corporate team based in Brussels. Over 30,000 organisations use the EFQM Excellence Model and research shows that 60% of Europe's largest companies use the EFQM Excellence Model to improve their business performance. –See more at www.efqm.org.

The History and Origins of the EFQM Excellence Model

1950: In the early 1950s, the Union of Japanese Scientists and Engineers (JUSE) instituted the 'Deming Prize' to recognise both organisations and individuals who had made an exemplary contribution to the performance and Excellence of their organisations. While the Deming Prize is undoubtedly the first recognisable 'Excellence Model', its use as an internal Self-Assessment process, within global organisations was generally low outside Japan.

1983: In the US a White House Conference on Productivity was held, with keynote speeches from President Reagan, Vice President Bush (Snr.) and Commerce Secretary Malcolm Baldrige. The report published following the conference opened with a very blunt headline statement: "America is the most productive nation in the world, but its growth in productivity has faltered. A long and wide-ranging debate ensued, and resulted in agreement from both political and business leaders that a corporate performance Excellence should be recognised through the establishment of a highly prestigious national award presented annually by the President. Thus, the Malcolm Baldrige National Quality Award (MBNQA) was launched in 1988. It is now called the Baldrige Performance Excellence Program (BPEP)

1988: The Presidents of 14 European companies came together to create the then called European Foundation for Quality Management. EFQM, as it is now known, was formally established on 15 September 1988 in Brussels at the Chateau of Val Duchesse; where, thirty years earlier, the European Economic Community had begun. The Presidents of Bosch, BT, Bull, Ciba-Geigy, Dassault, Electrolux, Fiat, KLM, Nestlé, Olivetti, Philips, Renault, Sulzer and Volkswagen attended this important meeting and became the founders of EFQM.

1991: The EFQM Excellence Model was born. From 1988 to 1991, the newly established EFQM focused its activities on and around the development of a member network and the creation of the EFQM Excellence

Model. The work brought together a small core team of 10 so called "thinkers" supported by approximately 300 in-company experts from across the globe consisting primarily of the founders and early key corporate members of EFQM. The criteria for the EFQM Excellence Model were developed by taking the best from other business standards and models, including the Deming Prize, the MBNQA process and through lengthy consultation with leaders in the business community. The criteria established by this approach thus reflected a consensus of what best practice looked like at the time (and has been maintained by periodic reviews ever since).

1992: The first European Quality Award was presented, to Rank Xerox, by the King of Spain at the EFQM Forum in Madrid. This process has continued and multiplied every year, to date.

EFQM and its Networks today

Since 1991 agreements have been made with National and Regional Not-for-Profit Excellence organisations who now also operate a range of National and Regional Awards around the globe and provide a range of services often including translation of the Model and other publications in the local language. A full list of over 30 EFQM partner organisations, in a number of partnership categories, can be seen at ww.efqm.org and may provide valuable local support for you and your organisation.

Notes

Lightning Source UK Ltd.
Milton Keynes UK
UKOW06f0240080914

238150UK00002B/44/P